A VIEW
FROM THE
PACK

A VIEW
FROM THE
PACK

Swim, Bike, Run: 20 Years of *Tri*-ing

Dan Montague

A View From The Pack

Book design and layout by Jim Goold

Dan Montague
P.O. Box 26694
Fresno, California 93729-6694

Printed in the United States of America

ISBN: 0-9767301-0-3

First Edition

Contents

Acknowledgements

Thanks to travel buddy and fellow swimmer, Jim Goold for his technical expertise and advice in setting up this little book. Without his help and experience, this work would never have been finished.

Thanks also to Holly Chohan, my neice and upcoming triathlete, for her time and effort in editing and typing.

And many thanks to my friends and fellow triathletes John Devere, John Browning, Jim Harris, Mary Lou Hicks, Jim Manfredo, Steve Meunier, Dot and Larry Owens, Annie and Pat Phillips, Pat Monahan, Ron Ottaway, Barbara Anderson, Faron and Heleen Reed. They have all added much to the fun and fellowship of triathlon as we pushed and pulled each other while we all trained and raced together.

Lastly, a big *Thank You* to race promoters such as TriCalifornia, J&A, LA Triathlon Series, Onyourmark, and Sierra Multisports Productions. You guys likely hear a lot more complaints than praise. None of this would happen without your work and dedication, and for that, you have my gratitude.

1

The Early Years

I must have been born to do it. I started when I was nine months old, and at age 62, I'm still at it.

The author's father
George Montague on the
Mississippi College track team
c. 1930

IT… is running. My mother told me that I began walking at nine months, and the following day I started running. It is something I have always done and what I enjoy doing most. At least some of my ability must be genetic. My father was a sprinter in college, and one of my uncles was conference champion in the two-mile.

In the fifth grade, my teacher commented that she wished I was more interested in sports. The problem was she wanted me to be involved in team sports. At the time, I was more interested in marbles. In the sixth grade, I did get involved in football and basketball during the fall and winter, and in the spring I discovered track and I was "off and running," so to speak. Mrs. Vineyard would have likely been shocked to hear that the marble player turned into a lifelong competitive athlete.

My sixth grade teacher Warren Pruitt was a man in his late twenties who had been an athlete throughout high school and college. He brought to me a whole new enthusiasm for sports. We went to three track meets that spring and I placed in every race I competed in. There was another kid on the team who was always faster than me, so I always came in second, but I thought I was a real stud anyway.

All through Junior High and High School there was one person consistently faster than I was, my long time friend and competitor Nick Shubin. Nick and I started the first grade together and were schoolmates throughout high school. We both ran the 880. He was naturally faster and stronger than I was, but that was OK because he was a friend. In our junior and senior years we both placed in the league meets. Nick finished second as a Junior and first as a Senior, I was fourth and third, respectively. Nick went on to UC Santa Barbara and competed on their track team in the two-mile.

Torch Relay - 1960 Winter Olympics

During the winter of 1960, I was chosen to carry the flame in the Olympic Torch Relay for the Winter Olympics held that year at Squaw Valley. The relay began in Los Angeles and worked it's way north through the Central Valley. One runner was chosen from each high school in Fresno County, and I was lucky enough to have been selected as the representative from Kerman High. Each of the runners carried the torch about a mile along Highway 99. My mile was somewhere between Selma and Fowler. At the time, I thought the torch relay would be the greatest thing that would ever happen to me. Fortunately, even better things were yet to come.

2

The College Jock

After graduating from Kerman High School in 1960, I enrolled at Anderson College in Anderson, Indiana, a small Christian NAIA school. There, I made both the cross-country and track teams. Cross-country came as quite a shock to me. In High School, our training was fairly laid back and I doubt that I had ever run more than three miles continuously. We didn't even have a cross-country team. I discovered that a cross-country race was four miles long and I had only two weeks to get ready for my first race.

Our coach that year was a Biology instructor who had apparently run at least one race sometime in his life, and therefore was more qualified to coach than anyone else available. As you can imagine, the coaching was rudimentary. It mainly consisted of, "Run harder!" I later learned that the coach was paid only $50.00 for the season, and the entire budget was a whopping $150.00. At any rate, I survived my first season. I was usually the last finisher on our team, but at least I was into the system. More importantly, I learned to really enjoy long runs, either with team mates or alone. The fall colors in Indiana were beautiful that year, and it only rained occasionally on races.

Our first race was a home meet and was scheduled so that we finished in front of the home side bleachers during half time of a football game. I was in miserably poor running condition and completely inexperienced in the sport, and of course finished dead last. After crossing the finish line I assumed the standard hands-on-knees position, facing the football field with my backside to the several hundred fans in the stands. Only later did I realize that the running shorts issued to me had a large rip in the rear. I was the butt-end of the race and I proved it to everyone there. It took several weeks for me to hear the "end" of it from my new college friends. Although I made the team, I didn't earn a letter for the season.

After cross-country season ended we did little or no training until January, when we started weight training to prepare for track. I had never lifted weights before, so it was another new experience. This was my first year eating away from my mother's table and I thought I was slowly starving to death. As it turned out, I actually gained ten pounds that winter while doing weight training. Starvation wasn't imminent after all

In February we moved out to the track. Unlike the San Joaquin Valley, Indiana does have snow in February, sometimes quite a lot of it. The first day we sloshed through four inches of slush and ice water. I don't remember what workout we did that day, but I do remember that every step caused a big splash - and there were lots of steps. We had been told to wear two layers of sweats for the workout so we stayed fairly warm, but we were still miserably wet. Our coach that year was a man named Bob Wood, a competent coach. He knew when to yell and when to stroke, and he worked us hard. He kept up a continual banter with us and we all liked him, and worked hard for him. If any one wasn't feeling well, all you had to do was let him know and he would let you call it a day. Unfortunately, Coach Wood was with us only one year, then moved on.

The first meet of the 1961 season was the DePauw University Relays. I was scheduled to run one leg of a two-mile relay in which each runner runs a half mile. I ran the third leg, and by the time my turn came up we were way behind. I ran very poorly and finished even further back. I ran so poorly, that for the next meet, a dual meet at Indiana Central in Indianapolis, I wasn't even scheduled to compete in the 880, which was supposed to be my specialty. I was very disappointed and talked to the assistant coach, telling him I knew the race at DePauw had been ugly but I was capable of better and wanted back in the 880. He said he would talk to the head coach and see what he could do. It worked, they put me back in the 880. When we arrived at IC the next day I discovered that I had to race the runner named Scheidt, who had won the conference the previous year. Now I was really worried. I warmed up, all the while trying to calm myself down. When the gun went off, I got on Scheidts' back and hung there for the first 700 yards of the race, then was able to out-kick him to the finish. I had won my first collegiate race. The assistant coach came up and said me he was proud of me for producing what I had promised to do. That one race established me as Anderson's top half miler, a position I was able to hold for four years.

Later in the season we went to Purdue University for a four way meet with Purdue, Ball State, and Butler. I was a graduate from Kerman High School, an eighteen year old freshman attending little Anderson College, and now I was about to compete against a Big Ten team. I remember when we arrived at the university, the first building I saw was the High Voltage Lab, it alone was bigger than all of AC. To change clothes, we had to walk through a locker room the size of a football field to reach the back corner reserved for us. To make things even worse, I learned that Dave Mills, who had recently set the indoor 440 world record, was running the 880 that day. Talk about feeling insignificant; I was the country mouse in the big city. I warmed up despite the cold, raw, windy spring day and finished fourth. Mills was beaten by a teammate, and someone from Butler finished third. I felt some vindication.

1961, my sophomore year, was fairly uneventful in cross-country, except that I lettered and received the second year award - a white letter sweater. About all that happened in track was a pulled quadricept muscle and only one race that season. 1962, my junior year of cross-country, was much better. In a couple of races I ran very well and placed higher than expected. Again I lettered, and received my third year award; a black letterman's jacket. I was accused of wearing that jacket continually for the rest of the year. That simply was not true. I took it off for church on Sundays, and only slept in it once a week. The track season went very well. I bettered the school record in the 880 by four seconds although, due to a technicality, was not actually given the record.

My final cross-country season of 1963 went fine. We had an excellent new coach, Bob Freeman, and a much larger and stronger team that year. Our team won several dual meets and placed well in the conference meet. That year I didn't letter because of the stronger team. Track was a sweet success. I won every race against conference competition, finally got the school record, was voted captain and most valuable player by my teammates, and was also was named to the All-Hoosier Conference team. They didn't retire my number, but I did hear in a roundabout way that one of the coaches said that I was the hardest working runner he had ever coached - that really meant a lot to me.

Among my many memories from that season, two in particular stand out. The first occured early in the season during a home meet against Indiana Central. To understand this story you must know that the city of Anderson tested their air raid/storm warning sirens every Saturday at noon. The 880 was run at about 11:30 and I won the race and set a new school record. The meet continued until about 11:55 when a very heavy storm cell moved in. It was almost as dark as night. The wind howled, lightening flashed, and the rain poured down in sheets, flooding the track. At 12:00 noon the siren was tested as usual, right in the middle of the storm. Someone yelled "TORNADO!" Everyone looked for any shelter possible. I saw someone dive into a shallow ditch. In all the confusion I happened to see a parked car with an open door and jumped in with about eight other people; there we sat out the rest of the downpour. In a very short time it was all over. There had been no tornado, just a quick, wet storm and a siren test. We all soon collected at the finish line only to hear that the rest of the meet had been cancelled due to the flooded track. The coach saw me in the crowd and came over saying, jokingly, that I still couldn't have the record because the meet hadn't been finished. He knew I had complained at length about being denied the record the previous year and was having some fun at my expense. He was kidding - the record was mine.

7

The other memory that stands out needs a little explanation, as well. At AC we had Career Days every year, at which time prospective high school seniors that were interested in attending college there came to visit and learn more about the campus. Career Days always fell on the weekend prior to the conference meet. The seniors arrived Friday afternoon and went home Saturday or Sunday. During the weekend, one of the visitors came down with the measles. I must have had contact somehow, because the following Tuesday I broke out in a red rash and had a slight fever. I was beside myself. It only was four days until the conference meet, I was undefeated in that conference, and now I had the measles. It was actually a very light case and I didn't feel too bad, but after going to see the college nurse, she only confirmed the obvious: *It looks like measles.* I explained the situation to her but received no sympathy. "You better forget about the race, it's just not worth the risk," she said. I felt that decision should be mine to make, but nonetheless I had to have her clearance to run the following Saturday. I stewed and complained, and waited. On Friday afternoon I called her at the clinic and told her I felt much better, although I still wasn't feeling well. She relented and cleared me to race.

On Saturday morning the team headed south to Hanover College, which is beautifully situated on a bluff overlooking the Ohio River. Within minutes after our arrival, the competitors began showing up to express concern about my measles situation, and check for any "damage." I warmed up and felt OK, but not great. The start was staggered around the first turn and then we all broke for the rail. It turned out to be a tactical race and no one wanted to take the lead, so everyone held back going into the second turn. This likely worked to my advantage because I didn't have to spend much energy in the first three hundred yards. Finally, just as we went into the turn, I picked up the pace and moved into the lead. No one challenged me on the straightaway, so I held the lead around the third turn. Coming onto the back stretch, Bob Miller from Hanover moved up to pass and I almost let him go. At the last possible second I woke up and decided to force the decision then and there. I picked it up a bit and we sprinted down the straightaway, shoulder to shoulder. He broke as we went into the final turn and faded to third by the finish. I came out of the turn far enough ahead so that I couldn't hear footsteps; I knew I had the win. That was the supreme moment of my life up to that time. All the training had paid off! Victory was mine! Very quickly, reality returned. As I crossed the finish line I realized my legs would not hold me up and I was about to eat some cinders. Fortunately, a teammate was standing just past the line and I managed to grab him to keep from going down. The legs soon started working again and everything was OK.

The nurse had said the race wasn't worth the risk involved; even forty years later I totally disagree. Life is full of potholes. Take your chances to win when you get them, those chances may never come again. To this day, I wouldn't give up that moment for anything.

A final note about the conference meet. The mile relay was still to come. Indiana Central had by far the best relay team, and we knew we couldn't ordinarily beat them. Providence smiled on us again. Apparently IC's second leg runner didn't want to run against me

again as he usually did and traded places with their third man. Maybe it was due to handing off to a different man, but IC dropped their baton on the three to four exchange and the baton landed out of their lane. They were DQed. We had finished second after IC picked up the baton and repassed us, but we were given the gold medals because of the DQ. That dropped baton cost IC the conference championship, which was won by Taylor University.

The author finishing the 880 on the Anderson College track - 1964

In the weeks following the

9

conference I developed sore bumps on the back of my head and felt generally rotten, but managed to survived with no long term problems. Finals came and went and I was finally finished with college. I had to hang around for the graduation ceremony, but my best running buddy Larry Ditty was heading home the next day for his summer break in Pennsylvania. We both knew that our three year friendship at Anderson was just about over, and decided to go for one last run. I still wasn't 100%, and we only went about a mile, but it was great to get that last run in.

3

The Lost Years

I graduated from college in 1964...

...started a career as a Medical Technologist...

...ran the family farm...

...enlisted in the National Guard...

...it was a busy but uneventful seven years for me. I was just too busy making money to have any fun. In 1971, I decided to do a seven day backpack trip and knew I had to do something to get in better shape. During the 1960s, very few people were running for recreational enjoyment. I ran on and off for a few years but didn't really keep up a regular training schedule. As it turned out, I had done enough running to allow me to survive the backpack trip and, after returning home, I was determined more than ever to keep

running and stay in shape. I
learned that you have to make
time for what is really important.

After the pack trip I continued
running and was enjoying it
again. During the summer,
running in the evening was
possible, but in the winter, I
was only able to run at night.
Sometimes in the darkness and
fog it was a little difficult to see,
but I was familiar enough with
the terrain around the farm and had no problems. One night I failed
to see an empty glass bottle and hit it a glancing blow as I stepped
down. I was very fortunate not to have stepped directly on it.

The author (right) at Ft. Ord - 1966

In the Spring of 1972, an article appeared in the local paper about
the Morro Bay Rock to the Pier 10K race. I signed up for the event
and now began to train seriously for it. Up to that point, I had been
running only a mile or two three or four times a week, obviously not
enough to get ready for a 10K race. I was running in an old pair of
training flats left over from college, with very little cushioning. With
the increased mileage I was putting in, my feet blistered over and
over again. There were now several layers of blisters on the bottom
of my feet to deal with. At the end of the race, a friend saw my feet
and asked if the race had done that. I had to tell him, "No, that's
from training!" After the race was over, I was addicted to running
again. It was that summer during the 1972 Olympics that I watched
Frank Shorter win the Olympic marathon; now I was really hooked.

I did 10K races, half marathons and finally full marathons. I trained
harder and harder, and unfortunately succeeded in blowing out
an Achilles tendon. After two or three months I was able to run
again, but the Achilles remained a chronic problem for years. The
newer, better designed shoes that were becoming available did help,
orthotics helped, but the chronic problem never completely cleared
up; the cycle just kept repeating itself.

13

4

Aconcagua

First View of Aconcagua

A longtime personal goal had been to climb above 20,000 ft. During the middle seventies I had climbed Kilimanjaro (19,340 ft) in Tanzania; Cotopaxi (19,344 ft) in Equador; the Mexican Volcanos Popocatapetl (17,887 ft) and Orizaba (18,855 ft). In 1982, I signed on with Rainier Mountaineering, Inc. of Seattle to do a trip to 22,834 ft Aconcagua in Argentina. Information from several sources indicated that, while Aconcagua is not an extremely technical climb, the altitude and frequent storms make it a formidable undertaking. I had done two previous climbs with RMI and had been very impressed with the quality of leadership they provided. I decided to go with them again.

Training for the climb didn't go well at all. The old Achilles problem was still with me and had reduced my running to just one mile, two or three times a week, with a little bicycling thrown into the mix. Three weeks before the departure date I came down with a particularly nasty cold that refused to clear up and resulted in an ear infection. This of course finished any training during the last weeks before the trip. In the end I had to leave with the cold and hope for the best.

Eight of us met at the Braniff desk at LAX. Although most of us wore slacks and jackets, it was easy to pick out the team members. The hiking boots, packs, and ice axes were a dead giveaway. The group included our guide John Smolich; Vladimir, born a Yugoslav - now a US citizen, was an anesthesiologist, and our team medic; Todd, an engineer working in Saudi Arabia; Ted, a German citizen living in LA, and at 46, the oldest person in our party; Mary, the only woman in the group; Paul, the youngest, at 26; John Perone, the only person who hadn't climbed higher than 15,000 ft, and finally me. We would meet our local guide Ramon in Santiago, Chile, and afterwards pick up an English climber who would join our group in Mendoza, Argentina. Of the group, only Ted and Perone had met previously.

February 4

We arrived in Santiago. At that time, General Pinochet was still in control of Chile and the police-state was very much in evidence. The downtown area of the city was crawling with police armed with either Uzis or sidearms, and they showed a sinister arrogance. They almost seemed to be daring anyone to cross them. We all managed to behave ourselves and keep quiet, and had no problems. We were all glad we didn't have to live in such an oppressive system.

February 5

We traveled over the Andes by bus. The mountains were simply

15

amazing. The Sierra's are to the Andes as the California Coast Range is to the Sierra's. We went over the Uspallata Pass at about 12,000 ft and into Argentina, then on to Mendoza to pick up our climbing permits. The bus was comfortable and the scenery spectacular. We stopped several times in interesting spots, and generally had a great day.

In Mendoza we were met by our last climber, Englishman Norman Croucher. Norm turned out to be an interesting and remarkable person. At age twenty-one he was involved in a train accident that resulted in the loss of both legs just below the knees. He now walks on prosthetic feet, and climbs with crutches. As he was recovering from his accident he decided to try to walk the entire length of Britain, partly to toughen his stumps and to help him recover from the depression he had fallen into. He was noticed by the British press, who reported on the progress of his hike and as a result was invited by some climbers to try an easy climb and one thing lead to another. By 1982, he had climbed all over the Alps, and in several South American countries. He currently makes his living working with various handicapped causes, and is a writer with several published books. He caused me to rethink my definition of what a handicap is and what handicapped people can do.

A few years and several attempts later, I was able to find a copy of Norman's book, *A Man and his Mountains*. It is part autobiography of his life, injury, recovery, and philosophy; and part travel log about his many climbing trips. I enjoyed the book a lot. It was an inspiring story of overcoming loss and self-doubt, as well as the doubt of others, and to go on to succeed in life. One of the chapters was about the Aconcagua climb. I enjoyed that too, it's fun to see your own name in a book. Something else that I found interesting was how much different peoples perception of one event can vary. More on that point later in the chapter.

February 9

Permit day! We had all heard horror stories about getting climbing permits to climb in Argentina, the red tape was terrible, they could refuse to issue you one on minor points, etc. All the stories were completely wrong. The office was in a beautiful, huge city park, and the people there were great. They were pleasant, helpful, cheerful, all the things we wish our civil servants (serpents) would be. We had scheduled a whole day for the process, but it was all taken care of that morning. We had the afternoon free, and our group made the most of it. Mendoza is a modern, well planned city, with tree-lined streets, parks, and nice shops. Most of us spent the afternoon walking, and lazing in sidewalk cafes. The steaks were tender, the service good, and the prices low by US standards.

At about 5PM, several of us were back at the hotel sitting on a shaded patio at the back of the hotel. Several rooms and a common shower opened onto the Patio. Just us guys were there, Mary was elsewhere. Soon, a particularly pretty and well-built señorita came along to use the shower. A few minutes later, Ted came wandering down with a towel over his shoulder, and headed for the same shower. None of us wanted to interfere, so we said nothing. The door wasn't locked and Ted went right in…and Ted came right back out again - with a sheepish grin on his face. We had a good laugh at Ted's expense and another chuckle when the pretty señorita reappeared in a few minutes.

February 10

To get to the trail head we had to drive back most of the way to the Uspallata Pass. Going to Mendoza to get permits, then back to Los Penetientes ski area wasted two days and at least 200 miles of travel, but is the way it's done. One final hurdle is to check in with the army and get their permission to be in the border area. At the time, Argentina and Chile were spitting at each other and both wanted to know who was in their territory. At any rate, Ramon had been in the military office, when he and a sergeant came out and walked up to the van we were sitting in. As the officer came to the side of the van, he reached down to his .45 sidearm and pulled it partway out of the holster, then let it slide back down. I don't think we looked threatening, but maybe that was his way of letting us know who was in charge. After that exercise in intimidation, he collected our

17

passports for the duration of the trip and sent us on our way.

Our outfitter for the climb was Fernando Grijales. He had been quite a climber in his younger days, pioneering several routes on Aconcagua. He has made his living ever since by providing mules, riders (arrearos) and local transportation for climbing parties. That night, his wife fixed dinner for us at their hostel. We started off with soup and salad, followed by empanadas (a delicious, spicy, fried meat pie), and ended with fresh peaches, all served with red and white Argentine wine. After dinner, Fernando gave us a slide show of some of his past climbing exploits. Great hospitality.

February 11

The first day of the approach march. We trucked to the trail head at Punta de Vacas at 7,000 ft, then headed up the Vacas River, which we were to follow for twenty-four miles. We walked 12 miles that day under moderate packs, on never ending broken rock of varing stability. Due to my cold, I wasn't in very good condition, I had a new pack which caused some sore spots; basically, it was a tough day. I tried to hide a nose bleed at the first rest stop, fearing that John Smolich would send me back down.

The Vacas River came directly from the glaciers above and was so heavy with grit and glacial flour that we tried to use smaller side streams for drinking water. These were a little cleaner. We filled pots with water and let them set until the grit settled, then treated it with iodine tablets. During the day, we had climbed 2,000 ft and set up camp at 9,000 ft.

February 12

The day started with a stream crossing! The river was twenty feet wide, waist deep, totally opaque, rocky, and boiling down the canyon at great speed. Other than that, a piece cake. Oh yeah, did I mention the water temperature is about 33 degrees? Not something you want to swim in, especially wearing a pack. Smolich went first with a rope and got it anchored on both sides. Then, we carefully

Perone crossing the Vacas River on approach - February 12, 1982

went across, one at a time, until only Norman and Ramon were
left on the other bank. Norman had prosthetic feet; this had both
benefits and detriments. On the positive side, his feet didn't get
cold in the freezing water, but on the negative side, the prosthetics
didn't give him any information about his footing and they had a
tendency to float to the surface, adding to the difficulty. He was very
apprehensive about the crossing, but it had to be done. Norman
entered the water with Smolich by his side, and after a few tense
minutes, made it across. We all celebrated! Finally, Ramon crossed
and it was all over.

It was another hard day on the trail, another twelve miles, another
two thousand feet, mostly on broken rock. By this time several of
us had "the trots." Perone said that he had his pants off so much his
butt was going to sunburn. Due to a misunderstanding, we had a
shortage of toilet paper. One of the guys claimed he was wiping with
gravel; he smelled like it. I only had a minor case myself, so only
"tanned my butt" a little.

19

Some of the group were feeling fine and set a very fast pace. The rest of us were having a hard time keeping up. Smolich yelled and fussed, but the jackrabbits kept sprinting off until John told them to shape up or he would make them stay behind him. That seemed to cool them down a bit. Perone, Paul, Norman and I were all slow and lagging. Norman said he could usually stay ahead of one or two on most trips, but here he was bound to be last. Actually, I was having a hard time keeping up with him. I'm not used to being at the back of the pack, and it was hard to deal with.

All things come to an end, and we finally got to our second camp at 11,000 ft. We were at the confluence of the Relinchos River, which we were to follow up to base camp the next day. This was where we had our first view of Aconcagua. The valley formed a perfect "V", like a gunsight, and Aconcagua was the bead. The air was perfectly clear, no clouds at all, and the Polish Glacier shone pink in the alpenglow. It was a magnificent view of the mountain, and revealed an awesome climb to come. The mountain appeared quite near, but in reality, we had several hard days and nearly 12,000 ft of climbing to reach the summit.

February 13

This morning we saw our first wildlife on the mountain, two Andean Condors and five Guanacos. None of us, other than Ramon, had seen either before, and we were amazed at the size of the Condors and the grace and agility of the Guanacos. I noted in my journal that just seeing them made the whole trip worthwhile.

The Relenchos was much smaller than the Vacas, which was fortunate, because we had to make multiple crossings that morning. It was never more than knee-deep and really didn't slow us down much. Each time it was the same drill. Take off the boots, put on running shoes (the rocks were too sharp to go barefoot, and even running shoes helped protect our feet from the icy water), wade across, take off running shoes, rub feet dry in the very dry air, put boots on. The canyon was steep and narrow and strenuous going, but it eventually opened up into a wide, nearly flat mesa. Here, there was a great view of Aconcagua; we all took photos, and a much needed break. While we were resting, two climbers came down the trail toward us. They were part of a group of five. One of them had developed altitude sickness and had to go down to rest at the 11,000 ft level. We didn't see these two again, but did see the other three as they came down the mountain. Two of them had summited.

We saddled up again and plodded on and ever upward, and finally arrived at base camp. Base camp is officially known as Plaza de Las Mulas, and sits at the head of the Relinchos Valley at an altitude of 14,460 ft. It is in a small basin about 200 yards wide, and the upper end is directly at the head of a glacier, out of which flows a small, clear stream. The creek water was judged to be pure enough to drink, which we did, without problem.

I had never been as tired as I was at the end of the days hike. I was so tired I ached. It was worse than after a marathon. It was my turn to cook supper, but I was too tired to even do that. We had walked 36 miles and gained 7,000 ft over very tough trails in three days. We needed a rest day!

February 14

Valentines Day, better yet, a rest day. We were all worn and sore. Everyone slept late, ate a lot, drank liters of water, and tried to wash up in the glacial runoff. The mules carrying our heavy gear and extra food caught up with us, so we had fresh clothes and the cold weather gear. We divided up bags of food and white gas for a carry to Camp 1 in the morning, sharpened our crampons, and checked our gear again.

By this time the climbing party has broken up into definite groups. Mary, Paul and I usually share one tent, Smolich, Norman and Ramon another, and Todd, Ted, Perone and Vladimir, a third. A constant flow of filth and dirty jokes came from the latter four; the rest of us called them "The Animals." Even after everyone had turned in, we could still hear the *Animals* laughing at yet another dirty joke. Someone asked Mary if she was bothered by all the filth.

21

She replied she wouldn't mind if it stopped. Mary complained to us that she wasn't getting any support from the guys, and went on to say that she felt that she was the weakest member of the group, and needed support, but added that she didn't expect anyone to hold her hand and carry her pack. After that, the smut decreased, but didn't stop entirely.

Mary said she was the weakest member of the group, but that wasn't exactly right. I had heard her mention on a previous occasion that she could carry a pack if she was able to lift it up and put it on without help. If she did need assistance getting it on, she would probably have difficulties later on. On this climb, she carried her share of the weight on every carry, which was more than some of us were able to say. Her comments were even more meaningful when we learned that a lot of her load packing had been up Mt. Rainier.

February 15

I stayed at base camp again today with Paul and Norman. At least for now, we were the weak links. It was hard on the ego to sit here and have others do work I should have been doing. I was used to leading a group and carrying the heaviest pack. It was a bitter pill to swallow. During the morning, the other three climbers mentioned earlier, came down past us. They stopped to talk for awhile, and among other things, complained about one of their team members who didn't do his share of the work. Paul, Norm and I looked at each other and wondered if the rest of our group were thinking the same thoughts about us. Later in the day, the seven came down from the carry; no one said anything nasty to us.

February 16

We moved to Camp 1 at 16,500 ft today. A lot of the time we were on very steep scree, and the going was tough, but it only lasted four hours and didn't seem as bad as some of the approach marches.

Up here we must pressure breathe occasionally to avoid getting a headache. In pressure breathing, you must take a deep breath, then force it out past pursed lips. This increases the back pressure in the lungs and results in more oxygen absorption. At one point while sitting there I felt lightheaded, but some pressure breathing cured it. The mountains here were awesome. Looking down the canyon I could see over the top of a 16,000 ft ridge, to the left was 16,800 ft Ameghino, above us were snow fields all around. A small stream ran near the tents. This was our last liquid water; from here on we would have to melt snow for drinking and cooking.

I wore my double boots for the first time today; they were not very comfortable, but necessary because of the cold. The boots were too stiff and didn't let my ankle flex laterally. I had a blister on each foot from the double boots, but had to live with them. Above 15,000 ft, climbing gets much, much tougher. I had said earlier that at base camp I was so tired I ached. Every day past base camp I ached within thirty minutes of starting, but there wasn't much to do, but go on. It was a revelation to me that even at this stage of exhaustion, I could still continue on. I was at a disadvantage because the cold was still bothering me, but I'm sure most of the rest of the group were feeling the same thing. No one said much about it, but I'm sure they hurt, too.

Uphill from Camp 1 to Camp 2

23

February 17

Another rest day for me. I, and three others, stayed at Camp 1 while six members carry to Camp 2. I really felt down about this whole thing. I still felt rotten, having laryngitis so bad I could hardly talk. I couldn't even help with the carries. The previous night I had talked to Smolich about going down to base camp. He said everything was OK and to just hang on and roll with the punches. John suggested I could contribute by having hot drinks waiting for the carry team when they returned. I did what he said and had coffee and tea waiting - it was much appreciated. I'm going on!

February 18

We moved up to Camp 2 at 19,000 ft this morning. As I was sitting at a rest break, a tiny hummingbird flew up and landed on the toe of my boot and sat there for a few seconds looking at us. We decided it was a favorable omen! I can't imagine what that bird was doing that high on the mountain. There hadn't been any flowers for 12,000 ft. After 10 seconds rest he buzzed on down the hill.

We reached Camp 2 at about noon. It was all you would expect a climbing camp to be. All three tents were crowed onto a narrow ledge only a few feet wide, with a vertical wall behind and a steep scree slope in front. The only sanitary facility is just around a corner of rock, almost out of sight. We were here for two nights, as the following day was another rest day. Across the canyon, glacier after glacier dropped into a 3,000 ft valley. A little to the south, a trickle of water has refrozen into a massive ice fall. Beyond the ridge stretched an Andean range, a jumble of peaks and glaciers as far as the eye could see. The wind was picking up and there was a little snow. Beautiful!

February 19

Another rest day. Not much to do but sit around and smell yourself. I had gotten pretty rank, but hadn't smelled any one else; maybe no one else stunk. Someone commented that it was nice to have a woman around. Perone piped up, "Yes, it makes us guys be more careful about our appearance." At the time, he had 10 days of black stubble on his gaunt, sunburned face, white zinc oxide on his nose and around his mouth, and a blue doo rag on his head.

It was very cold and windy the previous night, cold enough that I zipped up my bag completely for the first time. I slept in all my clothes except my boots and coat. At 19,000 ft, even brushing your teeth is a chore, and getting out of your sleeping bag, putting on your boots and coat and going out to the "facility" is a major effort.

John Perone being careful of his appearance

All of our water came from melting ice. The stoves didn't work very well at this altitude, and this morning it took until noon to melt enough for drinking and making lunch. Water was so precious that we didn't bother with washing up. When we cooked, we first made the main dish, which was immediately eaten, then we made soup with any leftovers as a thickener. Afterwards, we heated water for coffee or hot chocolate, even if it had any soup scraps still in it (we wasted nothing). Finally, we melted ice to fill the water bottles and anything in the pot went into the water bottles, which were then taken into the sleeping bags with us to prevent them from freezing.

The central topic of conversation was all of the wonderful things we were going to have to eat when we got back to Grajales's resort. Todd fantasized about more tender steaks, I was sustained by the thought of a plate of fresh hot empanadas.

February 20

We moved up to Camp 3 this morning. After only a few hundred yards it became apparent that Perone was not well. He was a little

25

incoherent, and Smolich could see it would not be safe for him to go any higher. Perone was still rational enough to understand that his climb was over and that he had to go down to a lower elevation to recover. He didn't argue, and started back down toward base camp right away. We all said our goodbyes to John, realizing that it could have any of us. It was really sad to see him denied a shot at the summit after all the training, expense, travel and hard climbing he had done. He was strong and healthy, but altitude strikes who it will, regardless of conditioning and strength.

After a further few hundred yards we reached the Polish Glacier. On the ice a couple hundred yards away were the bodies of three climbers killed earlier that year. There were two Americans and one Argentine, all inside sleeping bags to protect them from the elements and to keep them from thawing until they could be retrieved. Not a happy sight, but one that many climbers have had to deal with. They had been killed in falls higher up the glacier and had been skidded down as far as gravity and slick ice would allow them to go. The bodies were at nearly 20,000 ft, and at that elevation, carrying them down would be a hugely difficult effort.

After strapping on our crampons, we started across the glacier. At first, the grade was slight and the going easy, but it became more difficult as we neared the far edge of the ice. We were not roped up, and I was a little spooked at the thought of not having any protection other than my ice ax, but soon we were across and onto scree.

We found ourselves on the last visible area of any rock or soil before the summit. Maps had shown another camp area 1,000 feet higher, and off the glacier above were we had stopped, but for some reason we didn't try to get there before setting up camp. The area was a jumble of broken rock, and we wasted a lot of energy wandering back and forth trying to agree on a camp site. Ted even started excavating a small tent platform with his ice ax, which was soon abandoned as we moved yet again. All of us finally agree on a site, and pitch the tents in a rockpile, a very uncomfortable place to sleep! By the time we were done, enough energy had been wasted to have seen us 1,000 ft higher than we were, with a better chance at the summit the next day. At 20,000 ft, any wasted energy is a terrible loss. Smolich was not with us for most of the day, as he had gone part way back down with Perone. Had he been present, we would have likely been better organized. John rejoined us later in the day.

February 21

We tried for the summit today, but didn't even come close. At about 21,000 ft, some of us were lagging badly behind and had slowed the others down so much that it was clear there wouldn't be enough daylight left for anyone to summit and descend before dark. It was decided to retreat back down to Camp 3 to rest before deciding what the next plan of action was.

View from high camp - 21,500 ft

I have to admit that I was the weakest link on the glacier, though others weren't much stronger. I was later told that Ramon was disappointed at how poorly we had done; he was certainly entitled to feel that way. Ramon was an experienced Andean climber, and most of the rest of the group had not tried a climb of this magnitude before. I had done all I could and am sure several others had done the same.

February 22

Here we sat, trying to decide where to go from here. Part of the group wanted to establish a higher camp this afternoon and try for the summit again tomorrow. I'd had it and was considering going down if that was the plan. A compromise was reached. We would traverse around the mountain and try another route, called the Normal Route. It was supposed to be an easier and ice-free route. There was, however, one small problem. We had rations for only one day. If we went down to base camp, there would be no problem; but the new route/summit attempt and retreat back to base would take three days. We opted for another summit try and short rations. About noon we headed for the high camp on the Normal Route at 21,500 ft and arrived there after a fairly easy climb, with plenty time to set up camp before dark. Supper was our only meal of the day, consisting of a skimpy helping of mac & cheese with tuna.

The world's highest building at 21,500 ft

I mentioned earlier that recollections of events vary widely from one person to another. A case in point. To me, eating just one light meal a day for three days while climbing at 20,000 ft and higher is a BIG deal, but Norman Croucher in his book, *A Man and his Mountains* doesn't mention it at all.

Tempers were beginning to flare. Ramon stomped out of a tent muttering "Chileano go home." I never learned what set him off, but he fortunately cooled down and decided to stay. A wise choice, considering that it was nearly night, it was snowing, and a nearly fifteen-hour walk back to base camp. Even the *Animals* were quiet. We were all near exhaustion. Throw in the lack of food and the disappointment of the failed summit attempt; we had good cause to be grouchy.

The author at the summit of Aconcagua

February 23

"Made it to the top of Aconcagua. It was a real struggle but we all made it, very tired. Almost no food, little water. At the summit and all the way down in a snow storm. As soon as I got back to camp I just hit the sack. Everyone seemed to push themselves to the limit. Better tomorrow."

- *An excerpt from my diary.*

After a breakfast of one package of instant oatmeal each, we saddled up for another summit try. The first few hundred yards were easy enough but then the grade became tougher and we entered the infamous Canneleta, a rocky, boulder filled gully that seems to go on forever. The weather had socked in by this time so that visability was only a few hundred feet by the time we reached the top of the Canneleta. From that spot, just visable through the mist, were two rises which we thought were the top. The left rise was the higher of the two, so we headed for it. Ramon, Smolich and Norman were on top first, then Paul, then me, followed by Mary, Ted, Vladimir and Todd. We had done it. We were at the highest spot in the Americas,

29

22,834 ft. Congratulations were passed around, everyone signed the register, took a few pictures, and rested briefly. Due to the mist and the snow storm that soon developed, nothing of the panorama of the Andes could be seen. I don't remember feeling any sense of elation, just gladness to be on top and not having to go up any more. I did have one problem at the summit with my power of speech; I couldn't make meaningful sentences. I knew what I wanted to say, but after the first word, everything else that came out was gibberish. My body was telling me not to go any higher.

The summit was a relatively flat and smooth area of weathered rock about the size of two tennis courts, with a metal cross installed at the highest point. Smolich had a RMI flag to tie onto it, but I have no recollection whether he did or not. There was also a metal box containing a register which is signed by everyone who can get there. The cold and fatigue and diminished mental capacity resulted in some weird looking signatures. No one in the group had a thermometer, so we don't know how cold it was at the summit, but several of us had icicles in our beards. I had on six layers of clothing and was comfortable, but not hot. Those layers included three of wool, and a down parka.

After twenty minutes, it was time to retreat to the relative safety of our tents. As we started down, we found a trail we had missed on the way up and had an easy time of the descent. I remember stopping once to put on crampons and Smolich yelling at me for being so slow, but otherwise it was an uneventful walk in a snowstorm at 22,000 ft. It only took an hour to return to camp and the sleeping bags. I remember supper as being a handful of peanuts and a third of a candy bar. The scrawl in my diary was barely readable. Everyone was asleep before dark.

February 24

We came down off the mountain today. Snow was falling much of the time, the rest of the day we walked in a layer of fresh snow. We crossed the bottom of the Polish Glacier without crampons, then stopped briefly at Camp 2 and helped ourselves to a few candy bars which had been left there by some prior group, our first food of the day. We hiked through a howling storm on the way to Camp 1. The snow was falling heavily and the wind cut right through our clothes. At Camp 1, Smolich realized the group was getting very weak and needed to have some substancial food. More food had been cashed there, and Todd was able to start up a stove in spite of the storm, and Ramon cooked up some mac & cheese with some strange canned beef added into it. It was so bad that some of the people wouldn't eat it, regardless of how hungry they were. I, of course, had three helpings. The little stream at Camp 2 was still flowing, in spite of the cold, and we were able to get a real drink for the first time in days. After eating, we slogged on down the mountain and arrived at base camp about 11PM. The 7,000 ft descent took fifteen hours; it had taken us four days to climb up that same distance. There were cookies and hot chocolate at camp, but I was too tired to eat. I crawled into the sleeping bag and awoke the next morning in exactly the same position I went to sleep in.

February 25

The next morning when I tried to tie my boots, I realized the three outer fingers on each hand had huge blisters on them. Apparently I had taken my gloves off one too many times during the storm, and had a light case of frostbite. They didn't hurt, and I hadn't noticed them during the night. Vladimir checked the damage out, wrapped them with gauze, and said not to break the blisters until the fluid had reabsorbed. They were fine in a week, but did make quite a conversation piece for awhile. The only way we could think of to describe

Frostbite first aid - Aconcagua, 1982

31

them in Spanish was *Helados del manos*, literally "Ice cream of the hands."

We told stories, laughed, ate, drank, and generally enjoyed our success all morning. As the hours wore on we began to worry about Paul and Smolich who had stayed at Camp 1 overnight, as Paul was too exhausted to finish the descent that night. We were about to send up a rescue party when they popped into view over a ridge. As soon as they had rested a little and eaten something, we headed back towards civilization, walking twelve miles before dark. That evening, Mary volunteered to cook supper, since it was the last night on the trail. She made mac & cheese again, but somehow it was much better this time than all of the previous mac & cheese meals we had eaten.

February 26

We walked twenty-four miles under pack today, and didn't arrive at Punta de Vacas until after dark. Total exhaustion again. We came to the military chechpoint at the highway, and were greeted royally by the soldiers on duty. They gave us Mate and coffee and bread and seemed to be very impressed that we had gotten nine out of ten climbers to the summit of Aconcagua.

February 27

Back in civilization. A cot to sleep on, real food, cold drinks, showers (cold). Time to rest and think, and then rest some more.

I included this chapter on Aconcagua in my book because without the experiences and lessons learned on the mountain, I would most likely not have been able to train and race as a triathlete for the past 20 years. It was on the mountain that I found a much greater understanding of human endurance, and where I realized it was possible to go on working far beyond anything I had previously thought possible. It was on the mountain that I formulated my "Law of Thirds," which goes like this: when you feel tired, you have done one third of the work you are capable of. When you are so tired you ache, you have done two thirds, after that, you still potentially have another third left. The farther one gets into that last third, the tougher it gets. At the end is total collapse, or even death. Possibly Phidipides is the only person I have heard of that reached his ultimate exhaustion. Phidipides was the Athenian messenger who carried the news to Athens of the Greek victory over the Persian Army at Marathon. After relaying the message, he dropped dead. I have no desire to go that far, but I did learn on the mountain that the last third is there to be used if really needed. I also concluded that climbing all day above 20,000 ft is harder than anything else I have ever done.

5

Multi-Sport Racing

After completing the Aconcagua climb I felt rotten for about four months. I had lost 15 pounds and had very little energy; nothing seemed to work as well as it did before the climb. Eventually my strength returned and I was able to begin my training again, but the nagging Achilles was still "nagging." I was working full time in addition to farming 100 acres of grapes, so training time was very limited. During the next two years, my training was reduced to running two miles, two or three times a week. Hardly the stuff of champions.

During the winter of 1983, I met an attractive, athletic woman a few years younger than me, who was interested in doing multi-sport events. Her enthusiasm was infectious. We soon became good friends, and trained, competed, skied, biked, swam and hiked together for years. Without Mary Lou's example and ambition, I very likely would not have gotten into triathlon at all. We would often ride several miles from her house to a local park, run a few miles, then ride back to her house. That was my first experience with double training sessions. The rides grew longer and began to venture into the local foothills, and the runs became more intense.

In the spring of 1984, I entered the Turlock Biathlon. Race day was cold and windy. The wind wasn't a problem on the run, and I was able to make it through the six miles OK. The 30 mile bike segment began with a trailing wind, which made it easy; I could feel my legs regain strength as I rode. Things went fine until the course turned and we came around into the teeth of that nasty wind. Suddenly my legs felt heavy and exhausted. Riders were scattered out every twenty yards or so, as far as the eye could see. They were far enough apart that most of us weren't getting any drafting effect. I was hurting a lot, and the only thing that kept me from quitting was the belief that everyone else was hurting just as much as I was. After a few miles, the course veered slightly, the going eased a little, and I was able to finish. I finished back in the pack, but was content in knowing I had completed the race.

Later that summer I entered the Dual at the Dam Biathlon, held at Millerton Lake, ten miles northeast of Fresno. The nine mile run was on trails through the hills and around the lake shore, and was quite steep and rough in places. I found it was almost as fast to walk the very steep sections as it was to run them, it saved a lot of energy. The run was tough. I was happy when it ended and we got to the "easy" bike segment. My training had consisted of a lot of running and a little biking, thinking that would suffice. I learned that day that running doesn't nescessarily make you a better biker. Biking helps your run, but it doesn't seem to work the other way

Turlock Biathlon - 1984
Harlon Rincon, Behzad Setoodeh, Dan Montague

Do I have to get into that cold water, again?

around. The bike course was 24 miles with a few moderately difficult hills. After about 18 miles, I was so exhausted that I was forced to stop and rest for a few minutes. Once I caught my breath, I was able to finish - again in the middle of the pack.

I was enjoying my participation in biathlons, but knew there was much more out there. In January of 1985, I joined the Clovis Masters swim program. The group swam at the Clovis West Aquatic Complex at Clovis West High School, which is actually located in the city of Fresno, not Clovis (figure that bureaucratic boondoggle out). I could swim after a fashion, but still had a lot to learn. About the only thing in my favor was good cardiovascular strength. I had to learn freestyle, then breast stroke, then back and butterfly, breathing technique, kicking - basically, just about everything. Our coach at the time was Nancy Landis. She took the time to show me much of what I needed to know, and had the patience to keep after me until I got it right. The first day I swam, I needed to rest after each 25 yard length in the pool. That first day I probably only swam 500 yards total, but at least it was a start.

I soon learned that most of Fresno's triathletes swam with the Clovis Masters, and I started getting acquainted with some of them. One of the first people I met there was Jim Manfredo (generally known as *Fredo*); it has been a long-term friendship. Mary Lou Hicks joined the group at about the same time, as did Steve Meunier, another early, longtime friend. We all swam, as well as ran and biked together.

Larry Owens moved to town a couple of years later, and became a training partner and competetor. Larry and I are only 10 months apart in age, and so we are in the same age group for four out of five years. Both of us were quite evenly matched in ability, and both hated to lose. We had a very serious, but friendly rivalry which lasted for years. For some reason, we seemed to take turns being dominant. Larry would win most of the time one year, then I would win the next, then Larry the year after that. We called it the *Alternate Year Syndrome*. I met many other people in the sport over the years, and gained many friendships

6

Triathlon

My very first Triathlon was the Volunteer Tri in 1985, put on by Franz Weinschenk, a long time friend. It was centered around the pool at Clovis West High School, which was very close to my home, so I was able to ride my bike to the transition area. The race began with a six mile run, followed by a twenty-five mile bike, and finished with a 400 yd swim in the pool. No memories of the race remain except how tired I was at the end. My finish was well back in the pack, but I had completed the distance, which was the major worry.

At that point, I completely lost my mind. I entered the Cascade Lakes Triathlon at Cultus Lake, just west of Bend, Oregon. It was a Half Ironman distance. Then, to make things even more absurd, I signed up for a three day climbing school and climb up Mt. Rainier in Washington; all to start the morning after the triathlon. I didn't have a clue!!!

I did train hard to prepare for a long race, and physically, I was ready for it. Three weeks before the Oregon race, a Tri for Fun was being held at Millerton Lake. A friend suggested that it would be a good idea for me to do it because I had not done a tri in which the run was the last event of the race. The Millerton race was to be my first open water swim. In the all of the kicking, clawing and splashing of the mass start, I managed to suck down quarts of water, and choked so badly that I would have quit if there had been any place to quit to. Out in a lake, quitting places are scarce and I couldn't find one, so the only option was to go on. Once I got through the choking, the rest of the swim went fine, as did the bike and run. I thought, "Cultus Lake, bring it on!" Ah, the foolishness of the inexperienced!

Friday afternoon we arrived at Cultus Lake, tested the water, set up camp, and drove down to Bend to register for the race the next morning. At the pre-race meeting, it was announced that the water temperature of Cultus Lake had dropped from 70 to 62 degrees due to an afternoon wind; wetsuits were now recommended. Many of us participants didn't have wetsuits. At that early date in triathloning, few age-groupers had bought them. After the meeting broke up, there was a mad dash for the only sporting goods store in Bend. The full suits were already gone and the only thing I could find was a neoprene vest. Another person saw it at the same time I did, so we flipped a coin for it - he won. No vest for me. By the time we drove back to the campsite at the lake, a hard north wind was blowing and the temperature was dropping. I spent a long, restless night worrying.

Saturday dawned with the temp in the 40s and a stiff north wind howling. At the lake, the water temperature was now 58 degrees with a rough chop on the water. The weather was so bad that race management postponed the start one hour. Had the race started at the scheduled time, I would have likely tried it without a wetsuit, but with an extra hour to think, wisdom, or maybe it was fear, had set in, and I decided to sit this one out. It was a wise choice. Quite a few people started without wetsuits, and many of them were pulled out with hypothermia. I watched swimmers in wetsuits come into the transition area blue and shaking so hard it took them several minutes to unzip their suits. We declared the morning a lost cause and headed to Rainier.

The following day we went through the Rainier Mountaineering climbing school, and the next morning, hiked up to the RMI hut at 10,000 ft, where we spent part of the night. At about 2AM, the guides woke us, we roped up, and the group headed up the mountain, most of whom summited. Usually if the weather is clear (as it was that morning), the view from the top of Rainier is spectacular. Mts St. Helens, Adams, Hood, Baker were all clearly visible to us. A beautiful sight! Even without a race, the trip had been well worth the effort.

In 1985, no one truly understood how to train for triathlon. Many people had theories and ideas, but the sport was so new that none of us really knew what worked and what didn't. Some people grossly over trained and a lot of us under trained. It was pretty much hit and miss. Cross-training was the buzz word, but it became apparent that biking didn't make you a better swimmer, and swimming didn't do much to help your running. Cross-training gave you cardiovascular fitness, but to excel, a person needed to do multiple sport-specific training sessions each week. A lot of useful information began appearing in the triathlon magazines, a few books on training were available, and slowly, a body of knowledge began to evolve about the sport: intervals, hill training, weight work, rest days, hydration, nutrition, attitude adjustment, and equally important, finding time for all of the above. From necessity, each of us gained some degree of expertise in each of these areas. We have made much progress since the early days, and performances have improved greatly.

In 1986, I did eight triathlons, and felt that I had over-raced. These included the Volunteer, Millerton Lake, and Bass Lake Triathlons. In those days, I didn't keep any records of training and races, and thus I have only recollections to fall back on. That year was the first time that Bass Lake was not the national championship race, but it still attracted many of the best triathletes from California and beyond. I remember standing in line just behind Scott Tinley and being amused that the registration volunteer didn't know who he was. Dumb locals! At that time, Bass Lake was an end of season get-together and party for all of us tri-jocks. A chance to get together and tell lies and war stories about the years races and adventures. It remained just that for several years, but later faded and eventually went the way of all amateur-managed races. It has been sorely missed. I recall having a satisfactory race and ending the season on a positive note.

The next year, 1987, I flew to Phoenix, Arizona with Jim Manfredo and his wife Trudi to do the USTS race at Lake Pleasant. It was supposed to have the toughest run of any of the USTS races at the time, and it was not a disappointment. The hills were steep and frequent and the weather was miserably hot. The race started at 6AM, but the temperataure was still more than 100 degrees before we finished the run. Jim finished 14th and I was 21st in the 40-44 age group. We went to the awards ceremony where I noted that from where I was standing in the back of the audience, the 40 year old women looked almost as good as those in their 20s. Up close the wrinkles showed, but from a distance they all looked good. A fit body is a fit body.

I won my first Triathlon that year. Jim Manfredo and Jeff Chadwick, another local friend, decided to team up and relay the Millerton Lake Tri, which left the field to me. A win is a win, and I took it happily, even if I knew it was a bit tainted. The Millerton Lake triathlon has taken on four separate incarnations over the years. It was sponsored by the Eye of the Chicken group for several years, then died, only to be brought back by Golden Valley for a few more years, died again, was resurrected for one year by the Fresno State Triathlon Club. Then finally, these last few years it has been put on by Sierra Multisports Productions. I know of no other race that has come and gone so many times. I did the Castaic Triathlon that year

Bass Lake triathlon - 1988

for the first of several times, and finished the season again at Bass Lake.

1988 was a big year for me. I won my age group at the Volunteer Tri, a legitimate win this time. I had aged up into the 45-49 age group and had escaped competing against Jim Manfredo for 2 years, but another athlete, just 10 months my senior, had moved to Fresno the previous year. I was able to finish ahead of Larry Owens that day, but it was the start of a long, friendly, and spirited rivalry.

I am 6'2" and lanky, Larry is 5'8" and muscular. We are nothing alike physically, but very evenly matched athletically. I was slightly better at swimming, we were about equal on the bike, and Larry was a little better on the run. We both hated to be beaten. We swam together several times each week, did a long run each Saturday afternoon, and biked occasionally. Larry and I always kept a running tally of our personal competition each season, and we seemed to alternate being best. One year Larry won most of the time, the next year it would be me ahead. Most of the time we traveled to races together and had a very enjoyable time doing it. Larry is very intelligent, having a Ph.D. in Electrical Engineering, and is a Professor of E.E. at California State University, Fresno; but he always seemed to be willing to put up with my mental mediocrity.

Later that spring, I traveled to Lake San Antonio to do Wildflower for the first time. I entered the long course, which was a 100K race at that time. The swim was 2000 m, bike 81K, run 17K. I had never done a long Tri, and was more than a little worried about being able to finish. I arrived on Saturday morning just in time to see the short course (40K) start. Weather conditions were abysmal. The temperature was in the 40s, a north wind was blowing down the lake, creating swells of nearly three feet. By 1988, most triathletes owned wetsuits and were now wearing them at races. The starting area of Wildflower is in a protected boat ramp area where the water is calm for about a hundred yards, but beyond that point you are out in the main lake and get the full force of the weather. That morning, about 60 people were pulled out of the water by the rescue teams. Many were hypothermic, some had panicked as the big swells out in the lake hit them, some just decided it wasn't worth the risk and turned back. The race continued, although it must have been miserable riding in that cold wind.

On Sunday morning, those of us doing the long course had our turn. There was a little frost on the grass, but the wind had eased a bit, although it was still blowing, and the chop on the lake was down to about 12 inches. The water temperature must not have been very low since I was only wearing a sleeveless wetsuit and wasn't at all uncomfortable. I did experience a moment of panic when the force of the waves first hit me, but controlled it and settled into a rhythm going through the waves.

Monterey Bay triathlon - 1988

Coming out of the water and running up the long, steep, ramp and stairs to the transition area was a chore. I decided to wear an extra shirt while riding, and was glad that I did, as I was cold until nearly the end of the bike. I remember riding up the last big hill, just before passing the park entry gate, and being passed by a woman who was running. That didn't do much for my ego. The run was a matter of alternately running and walking. I was so far back that some of the aid stations had no volunteers left manning them as I passed by. I finally finished, and it was over. I had done my first long race!

The Wildflower winner that year was a fellow Fresnan, John Devere, another Fresno pro, Mike Meteyer, came in sixth. Devere was coach of the Clovis Masters program, and he and I co-led a Bible study at my home, so I knew him well and respected him for his work ethic and down-to-earth spirit. I was pleased to learn they had both done so well. I had camped with them the night before and thought I was walking in "high cotton" just being around them.

At the end of June, several of us Fresnans traveled to Monterey for the Monterey Bay Triathlon, another Half-Ironman distance race. The bay is always cold. The water temperature at start time was 52 degrees, cold enough to make your feet ache when you waded in. Once underway (and wearing a wetsuit), it wasn't as bad as I had feared. This was my first ocean race, and I was sure that "Jaws" had to be down there somewhere, so I had quite a start when suddenly I was face to face with a kelp head. The kelp didn't bite, and I continued on. The bike course consisted of two loops around Ft. Ord. I had marched many of the hills during basic training in 1966, and now I was riding them; riding was much more fun! The run that year went out to Sand City and back, then north to Pacific Grove, and finally back to the finish on Cannery Row. John Devere won, and Bryan Fehrenbach, another Fresno pro, finished second. Mike Meteyer also had a top ten finish. Again, I was a mid-packer, but happy to finish the distance in good form.

Bike transition area - Monterey 1988

In June of 1989, I entered the USTS San Jose race, which was remarkable in two respects. First, I became aware of Walter Radloff of San Jose, who was to prove to be a long time nemesis. Although I

44

was eventually able to defeat him in 2002, he trounced me the first forty-nine times we competed. When I actually did finish ahead of him, he was very gracious about it when it finally happened.

The second notable memory was the color of the water in Lake Cunningham that year, it was bright green. As I heard the story, the lake had an alga bloom and to kill the alga an aquatic herbacide had been used which resulted in the green-hued water. Oh yeah, there was a third thing - Metcalf! Other than "The Beast" in the Bahamas, Metcalf was the toughest hill climb in any triathlon. The grade was 11-13% and it went on and on for nearly two miles. About a forth of the way up was a flat spot, just twenty flat feet, then back to the hill. Possibly 20% of the racers walked and pushed their bikes, another 20% zigzaged up the hill, the rest of us grunted up any way we could.

I hated Metcalf that first year, but eventually concluded that it was a gift to those of us who trained on hills. What goes up must come down, so over the top was a sceaming downhill back into San Jose. If you could survive the ascent, and then the descent, you were likely to have a good race. The race finished with a slightly downhill run into downtown San Jose. Many fine athletes raced in San Jose every year, and it was hard to have a podium finish. I think I managed to break into the top five twice in several years of trying. Because the start and finish were several miles apart, buses were supplied to take us back to our gear and cars. Larry Owens met his future wife Dorothy on one of the buses; I managed to throw up in another of the buses - ah, yes.

In August, I flew up to Spokane for the Troika Triathlon. I had a cousin living in Moscow, Idaho whom I had been wanting to visit, and the race gave me an additional incentive to go there. I spent several days with my cousin John and his wife Gerri, where I trained a little, and ate a lot. After the visit, they drove me back to Spokane for the race. The 2000 m swim took place in Medical Lake, approximately 20 miles outside the city, then a 56 mile bike through the beautiful, rolling hills of the Paloose, and then back to downtown Spokane. The 13 mile out-and-back run followed alongside the Spokane River, as it flowed over gentle rapids. All

45

went well until about the 10 mile mark, then nausea struck. I walked and retched the last three miles, and finally finished, but not in the style I had hoped for.

Races in McFarland and Bass Lake rounded out another season. It had been an acceptable racing year, some good efforts, and some not so good.

Bass Lake - 1989

Earlier in the year, Larry Owens and I had traveled to Redding for a race up there. On the way home I made a comment about his performance, and I knew it was the wrong thing to say the second it came out of my mouth. I had not intended to be nasty, but I have to admit it sure came out that way. Larry didn't respond, but from the body language it was obvious he wasn't very happy. I payed for that offhand remark all of the next year. He must have trained extra hard that winter, because Larry came back and trounced me in five out of six races the following season.

1990 was a forgettable year for me. Training didn't go well, although nothing was wrong with me, physically. I did seven races, none were very inspiring, and I knew that much of it was my own fault. At the end of the season at Castaic Lake, I told Larry that he had beaten me fair and square all year. He had simply out-trained me. I told him that he would never do that again. He might beat me again because he was a fine athlete, but it would never be because he had trained harder.

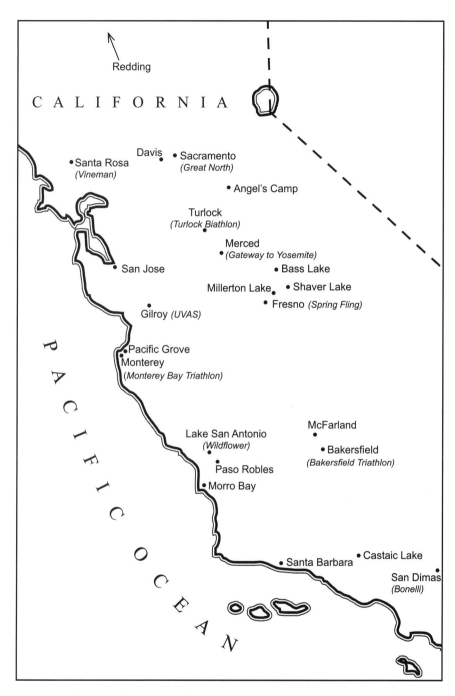

Locations of some California races that the author has participated in over the last 20 years

7

Vineman

I went to work with a vengeance that winter and the following spring, and so was better trained than ever to start the 1991 season. The major event of the year was July's Vineman in Santa Rosa. That year, the swim was in the Russian River at Guerneville, a 2.4 mi swim in cool, murky water. The course itself was beautiful, with Redwood trees lining the banks which provided shade in spots. In many places, spectators had come down to the bank to watch us, it was fun to watch them in return. It is unusual to have spectators near the swimmers, usually the swim course is in the middle of a lake. Toward the end of the swimming leg of the race, my hands were getting very sore from pulling through the water some 4,000 times. Actually, the swim is by far the easiest part of an ironman distance race. The best was yet to come.

Jim Manfredo and Dan Montague
Full Vineman, Santa Rosa - 1991

There were only four of us in the 45-49 age group, Jim Manfredo, me, and two others. By the time I transitioned to the bike, the others were long gone. The bike was as beautiful as the swim. It started with 12 miles riding through the Redwoods, then through Coastal Oak forest, to Geyeserville, where we crossed the Russian

River and rode for many miles through the vineyard country of the Alexander Valley, then turned west to climb Chalk Hill, then on down to Santa Rosa. From the north side of Santa Rosa, the course begins the second loop. Chalk Hill is reached at about fifty miles into the ride. The first time around it's no big deal. The second time, after about 100 miles of riding, it becomes a very BIG deal. The legs are aching, the spirit is depressed, the body is drying out, and that second time up is awful! I remember passing some recreational riders who were resting at the top and telling them how lucky they were. They were able to stop and rest. Once over the summit, several miles of gradual downhill awaited us, and a little recovery was possible. Then it was on to the transition area at the airport. I was certainly glad to be off that bike after 112 miles. Again, no one in my age group was in sight.

For a few miles the run went fine, but at about eight miles, the mother of all intestinal cramps tied my mid-section in knots. I had eaten several Snicker's Bars on the bike and likely the fat in the candy was causing the problem. I fortunately found a gully where I was able to get out of sight, and "rested." After that, I felt rotten for some time, and wound up walking most of the next five miles, but I kept going. At 13 miles I reached the turn-around, which was just across the airport from the finish. I briefly considered quitting and calling it a day, but when the moment of decision came, my body kept going and I was committed to finishing. I don't remember much about the last 13 miles. I ran some and walked some. I drank Pepsi at every aid station (one station even had ice in the Pepsi). At about twenty miles, a carload of teenagers passed by and gave me a big cheer, and that really helped keep me going. Jim Manfredo and his wife Trudi came out to about mile 23, which gave me a big boost just by them being there. Jim had finished an hour ahead of me, and had come back to help me in. Jim later told me that my whole face lit up when I saw them. I got such a charge from them that I did the last two miles in about 16 minutes, and finished feeling not good, but happy. Jim had finished third and I was fourth. No medal for me, but I had the finishers T-shirt.

In retrospect, the sugar in the Pepsi that I drank on the run most

Mary Lou Hicks at Bass Lake - 1991

likely enabled me to finish. Since high school, I have had problems with nausea during and after races. After years of trying to discover the reason, I realized that it must be low blood sugar causing the problem, with dehydration exacerbating the situation. I would get sick, throw up, then be unable to keep anything down. Without ingesting anything, the blood sugar stayed low and the dehydration factor didn't improve. It was a vicious cycle sometimes lasting for hours. I found that taking a gel packet before starting the run in an international distance race, and every hour in longer events, did help prevent the nausea. I also discovered it is critical to drink something along with taking the gel. At the Bakersfield Triathlon, there had traditionally been an aid station at the outlet of the transition area onto the run. One year, while anticipating a drink at the aid station, I took a gel before starting the run, but I soon found out that there was no aid station, and - no water. The first water available was two miles into the run. I finished the race well enough, but soon became nauseous. I was still throwing up gobs of that gel six hours later, and it wasn't until the next morning that I was able to keep anything down. There is a lesson here: know where the aid stations are. I have also noted that drinking water immediately after finishing the run helps. I began using the gel in 1998 and have not been sick since, except for the Bakersfield experience and a couple of very hot weather races.

In August of 1991, I flew back to Spokane for the Troika Half Ironman race. It was a hot, humid day. I swam well, had a flat tire and was able to fix it during the bike and wound up picking off a few runners on the out portion of the run. I knew I was getting overheated, and considered stopping to take a quick dip in the Spokane River, which flowed clear and cold a just a few yards away. A quick dip would have taken a couple of minutes, and I soon discarded the idea. As I ran through a shady spot a short while later, it felt like being in a refrigerator. I should have known I was in trouble. Shortly after that, at about eight miles, I started vomiting and fell apart completely. I sat down in a shady spot, and soon a doctor in a station wagon stopped to help. He got me into the wagon, put ice packs under my armpits and in the groin area, and hauled me in. At the hospital tent, they packed even more ice on me and started an IV (my first ever). It was amazing how fast that IV worked. With the help of a pretty, dark haired nurse named Ruth, and another doctor, I was soon feeling much better, and able to go back to my nearby hotel room. At home three days later, I received a phone call from the second doc. He was just checking to see if everything was all right. I was impressed!

Again, the season ended with Bass Lake. By this time, the race was losing much if it's early luster. The crowds were much smaller, the meals were no longer catered, and the competition was much poorer.

Dan Montague, Larry Owens, Dot Morse, and Steve Meunier at Wildflower - 1992

The race had changed management several times and it was on it's terminal slide, although it managed to linger on for a few more years.

In February of 1992, I did a trek in Chilean Patagonia. We hiked about 70 miles in eight days over varied terrain, and started with 80lb packs. The scenery was the equal of any in the world. Grasslands and forests, Guanacos and foxes, Geese and Megallanic Parrots, glaciers and waterfalls. Fantastic country. A great place to get into shape.

The early season went well, with races at Wildflower, Bakersfield and Millerton Lake, but early in June, that old Achilles problem reared it's ugly head. I wasn't able to run any more in June or the first week of July. I did, however, increase the bike distance considerably to take up some of the slack.

In June of that year, John Devere had hit a bump in one of our foothill roads and taken a nasty fall. He showed up at the pool with a sling to support his broken collarbone, multiple scratches and bruises, and road rash all over. Road rash is the result of scraping human skin across pavement at high speed. The only good thing about it is that every time you move during the next month, the pain lets you know you survived the crash. That particular bump was well known to all of us riders, as several people had crashed on it over the years. To prevent any future incidents, Jim Manfredo drove up to where the bump was, near the bottom of a steep hill, and painted it white with spray paint. Problem solved. A few days later, Jim was riding the same hill and got into a race with another rider he happened to meet. In the heat of competition, Jim forgot about his painted bump, hit it, and crashed himself. He, too, had severe road rash. Jim's doctor had him take a course of antibiotics to ward off possible infections, which slowed him down a lot.

About a week later, he and I did a 50 mi ride into the local hills. I was a little ahead of Jim when I heard brakes screeching, then a few seconds later a pickup pulling a camp trailer passed me, with a woman hanging out the passenger window screaming obscenities at me. To find out what had happened, I slowed down to let Jim catch up. As we were talking, I managed to get a little behind Jim and then bumped his rear wheel with my front wheel. In that case, the rear rider almost always kisses the pavement, and I did just that. I landed in the gravel on the roadside. Now three of us had severe road rash.

There is a saying among bikers that there are only two kinds of bikers, those who have crashed, and those who are going to crash. It was not my first time to crash, but the first time to have extensive road rash. We started calling it "road pizza" because after a couple of days, it looks just like a freshly baked pizza, all oozy and red with hunks of dead skin that resemble bits of baked veggies. I had been the only person in the riding group who didn't have scars on one or both hips, and now I had joined the club. A year later, I became bilaterally symetrical after another mishap.

At the time of my crash, I had been able to start up running again, but only 3 mi per outing. I missed only one training day after the crash and was back to all three disciplines in three days. It hurt for a few seconds when I got into the pool, but then was no real bother until the next swim. I did discover it was necessary to keep each area of rash covered while sleeping. If there was no bandage, the ooze would stick to the sheet, then pull off any scab that had formed when I rolled over.

On August 1, seven of us went up to Santa Rosa to do the Vineman Half Ironman. The group included Larry Owens and his wife-to-be Dorothy Morse, Barbara Anderson, Steve Meunier, Pat Monahan, Jim Manfredo, and me. We all stayed in the same motel and ate together the night before the race, and made a weekend of it. For several years, this same group raced, trained and traveled together. It was a close-knit bunch and we all had a lot of fun. Monahan posted the top time, Barbara and I both averaged 21.1 mph for the 56 mi bike, and I had a good run, in spite of my lack of run training. My time was 5:09, which placed third. On race day I was 49; if the race had been held two weeks later, I would have been fifty years old and would have won the 50-54 age group by 30 minutes. Oh well, "If a bullfrog had wings, he wouldn't drag his tail on the ground."

Vineman Triathlon - Santa Rosa, 1992
Left to right: Barbara Anderson, Jim Manfredo, Steve Meunier, Dan Montague,
Dot Morse, Larry Owens, Pat Monahan

By the time Bass Lake rolled around I had turned 50, and posted my first win in that race. None of the big guns of the age group had showed up, and someone asked, "Well, if no one is a threat, who's the threat?" I was fairly sure I was a threat, but not wanting to put a target on my back, I kept quiet. Although I won, the altitude and intensity of pace made it a hard race, considering my reduced running schedule.

1993 was my first complete year in the new age group, and I expected great things. Wildflower opened the season with me entered in the long course. It was a hot day, and as had happened so many times before, I fell apart halfway through the run. A sheriff picked me up for a ride back to the finish, and I shortly managed to throw up in the back seat of the vehicle. Down at the lake, I headed toward the hospital tent, and when I found it, I threw up again on the grass out front. A nurse saw me and charged out to tell me to quit puking on her grass. Great bedside manner! I was so disgusted by her reaction that I walked away thinking I would just find a tree, lie down and die where no one would harrass me.

I refused to go back to the hospital tent at Wildflower for years after that particular incident. However, the 2004 race happened to be held on a brutally hot weekend, and I finished the race severely dehydrated. I had drunk more than usual on the bike and run, but obviously it had not been enough. After finishing, I cooled off in the lake, but still felt sick. The hospital tent was my last resort.

A triage nurse met me at the door, listened to my problems, then found me a cot. A doctor started an IV, and a pleasant nurse watched over me. She even wiped my face after I threw up again. After two liters of IV fluid, I was feeling well enough for them to release me. The treatment I received was completely professional and caring. The hospital staff was swamped with sick athletes inside that hot tent, but all the while, they were very comforting and first-rate. The "Don't puke

Jeff Moffit at Wildflower - c. 1993

on the grass" incident must have been an isolated, even atypical event - something best forgotten.

The week after the '93 Wildflower I won at Bakersfield, followed a month later by a win at Millerton Lake, and two weeks later, a second place finish at San Jose. Things were going great! A few weeks after that, another win at Lake Sonoma.

July 31 was race day at Vineman. Normally, the coastal weather in July is overcast and cool. When I went out to my car at 4:30AM, the moon was shining and there was no fog at all. Things didn't look good! I knew we were in trouble when I could feel the sun burning through my wetsuit during the swim. On the bike, it got hotter and hotter; the sun was merciless and the humidity was high. At eighty miles I had to stop at the aid station and rest for a few minutes. The second time up Chalk Hill I had to get off and push the bike. I must have been off the bike for at least five minutes, but everyone else was also going so slow that I was only passed twice. It was reported that the temperature that day was 103-105 degrees, one of the hottest days on record in Santa Rosa. It was so miserable that less than 50% of the field finished the race. I was feeling awful at the start of the run, and didn't try to run more than half of the time. Doing a run-walk worked well for several miles. At about mile eight, I hooked up with another guy who was doing the same run-walk strategy, and we went along together for several miles. Soon, we were running more and walking less. If I had continued the easy pace, I might have finished, but we pushed the pace, and at mile 13, I was sick again and knew there was no point in going any farther.

Steve Meunier was out on the course watching for any of us who might need help, and took me to the hospital tent where they hooked me up with an IV right away. I have never quit a race because of exhaustion, but once I start vomiting, I know it's time to seek help. I went into the tent about 3PM and came out at 10PM. I soaked up 4 liters of IV fluid before I was able to pee. I wasn't able to keep anything down till the next morning. After the fourth bag of fluid, the doc checked to see if any of the fluid was going into the lungs. Fortunately, it wasn't. Finally, they released me and I was able to go back to my motel room.

The scene in the hospital tent resembled a MASH unit in a war zone. There were about 15 cots, and every one of then was full at all times. As soon as one was empty, another sick runner would stumble in and fill it. Everyone was throwing up or dry heaving. An IV changes the blood electrolite balance, and that causes violent shivering. The nurses were hunting for blankets to cover us with, despite the 103 degree temperature. As the evening wore on, an occasional athlete would finish, and in a few minutes, almost without fail, he or she would be helped to the tent to join in on the fun. I remember one fellow on the cot next to me had another pressing problem besides being ill; he and his wife were supposed to fly out of LAX at 6:30 the next morning. He was too sick to drive, his wife was exhausted, and they were faced with a 7 hour drive. They left the hospital tent at 10 that night.

The doctors and nurses were great. They were all volunteers and gave up their free time to help us out. Some of the athletes might have died without the care those good folks provided so cheerfully. Any care that an athlete receives in the hospital tent is covered by race insurance. If an actual hospital is needed, the athlete must take care of that bill.

Three weeks after Vineman, I traveled with Pat Monahan to Davis for a race. I was leading at the end of the bike, but lost a few minutes in transition because someone had moved my running shoes. I finally found them and began the run, only to be passed two miles later. I finished second, and would probably not have won, anyway.

At Bass Lake in September, I had a two minute lead nearing the end of the bike, when the bike chain broke. Larry Owens passed me to take the lead, then dropped out on the run due to a muscle injury. A second bike passed me, and he eventually won. I tried to push and coast into the transition area, but lost so much time that I knew I couldn't win, and bagged it.

A win at Morro Bay ended the season. I was very satisfied with five first place finishes, and two seconds.

8

Equipment

At the time I first competed in triathlon (1985), the equipment was pretty simple. Running shoes had already undergone major improvements in the 1970's, and in my opinion, haven't improved much since then. There have been many new models and ideas since the early days, but they really don't do much more for the runner now than they did twenty-five years ago. Wetsuits, on the other hand, have gotten much better, along with a gross increase in price. The first suit I tried was a surfing garment that wasn't really suited to triathlon. It was stiff around the shoulders and generally lacked flexibility, it was not comfortable at all. I soon replaced it with a suit especially made for triathlon; it was a huge improvement. Advances continue to be made, and each new year seems to bring something new to the sport marketplace. Another innovation that was of great help to me were the swim goggles with corrective optics. My vision is poor, and lenses of some type are a must. Contacts just didn't work out. For the first three years of swimming at the pool, I wore standard, non-corrective goggles. I got along, even managing to do open water races, but it was a struggle to keep on course. Eventually, I discovered corrective goggles. It was only then that I learned the black lines on the pool bottom weren't painted on, they were actually lines of small black tiles. I could now see buoy lines and markers as well. Sometimes it's the little things that make life easier.

The real revolution has come in tri-bikes. The earliest races were ridden on ten speed steel-framed dinosaurs with standard drop handlebars, weighing twenty pounds or more. Over the years, great advances have been made in braking and shifting systems, nine and ten gear clusters have become available, and tires have improved. The real breakthrough came in the area of aerodynamics. Aerobars significantly reduced the wind resistance of a human body passing through the air. Disc and deep-dish wheels, along with bladed or oval spokes, have all contributed to drag reduction as well. Frames are now made of aluminum, titanium, carbon fiber, as well as improved steel alloys. These new frames can be made more aerodynamic than the old ones, in addition to being much lighter; my newest bike weighs only 17 pounds.

Many new hydration systems have been introduced on the market, some of which work and some don't. Step-in pedal bindings have replaced strap-on models. Helmets have gone through myriad designs and fads. The bells and whistles have gotten lighter and more complex, much more expensive, and to some extent, you really *can* buy performance. However, the fastest, quickest and only reliable way to buy performance is with SWEAT. There is absolutely no other way to succeed in triathlon. You must train, or you will fail.

For those new to the sport, I offer here a few ideas and suggestions about equipment which will come in handy. Most of these are from personal experience, and perhaps a little personal stupidity!

1: Don't try to get that last mile out of your tires. As the tires get thinner they are more apt to puncture, and will cost you more in discarded tubes than you will save in the long run.

2: I quit trying to patch punctures in tubes long ago. About half the time the patches won't hold, and you never know which half you have until you are out on the road. Your best bet is to put a new tube on the bike for peace of mind.

3: Always carry some folded paper money when you go out for a ride. In case of a large cut in the tire, you can fold a dollar bill and use it as a boot between the tire and the tube to cover the hole. The bill is strong enough to keep the tube from bulging through the tire gash.

4: Carry a couple of gel packets on long rides. We all bonk out sooner or later, and they will give you the needed boost to get home.

5: Carry a CO2 cartridge and valve adaptor instead of a bike pump during races. It is a quicker and lighter alternative for fixing a flat tire.

6: Always carry two or more spare tubes with you during training rides. At least twice I have had three flats on the same ride. It doesn't happen often, but pushing a bike on foot for ten miles to get back home takes a while. The small added weight of the extra tube on the ride is worth it.

7: Carry a small repair kit which includes appropriate wrenches, a patch kit, and tire levers. Don't leave the pump at home.

8: After you fill your water bottles for the ride, don't forget to put them in the bottle racks on your bike. When you are out on a ride and the temperature is 103 degrees, a bottle forgotten on the kitchen sink doesn't help you much.

9: Never use your middle finger to communicate with rude drivers.

10: Buy a new home atop a 500 ft bluff with a 9% grade driveway, then do multiple hill repeats both running and biking. You will be exhausted (and broke), but you will be one tough triathlete.

11: After you set up your gear in the transition area at a race site, pick out terrain features (trees, buildings, flags, etc.) to help locate your spot when you need to. Every second in transition counts; time used to hunt down your equipment is time wasted.

12: When you expect to be swimming/racing in sub-60 degree water, it is wise to use a neoprene hood to limit the heat loss through your head.

13: Don't try to hold on to your running shoes too long. If you see wear in the tread layer that has gone through to the white sub-sole, it's time to invest in a new pair. Any time my feet start hurting, the first thing I do is change to a new pair of shoes. I can usually get about 500 miles out of a pair of shoes, your mileage may vary.

There is one other article of triathlon equipment that is common to almost all races. The porta potty! Races are generally held in locations that are totally inadequate to handle the elimination needs of hundreds, and sometimes thousands of nervous, well hydrated, carbo-loaded people. The solution to this problem is the porta potty - dozens of porta potties. Generally, they are situated downwind from the transition area. If the wind shifts, good luck. The lines begin to form about an hour before start time. Triathletes must be unusually well organized, because they invariably form one or two lines and wait their turn. There may be two hundred people in line, but they all wait patiently for their turn. Finally, the goal is reached, then it is time to actually go in. The floor is usually wet, the tissue is often gone (prudent people carry some of their own, just in case), and the smell is overwhelming, but you lock yourself in, anyway. You escape as soon as possible and race to fresh air. The porta potties are placed as close together as possible, and so you can hear what is going on all around you. Oh well, we all have to go through the same thing, and everyone needs a little humility once in awhile.

9

The Beat Goes On

Dan Montague and Steve Meunier
at Spring Fling

The 1994 season opened in early April with the Spring Fling Biathlon in Fresno's Woodward Park, and Wildflower, which was held later that month. That year, I had agreed to relay the long course with Jim Manfredo (runner) and Rhonda Hansen (swimmer). We finished third in our division and were pleased with the effort. The following day, I did the short course, and paid the price for racing two days in a row. I finished fourth, but had to dig deep to do so.

In May I went to San Dimas and did the Bonelli Park race, which I enjoyed so much that I have gone back nearly every year since. It is a moderately difficult race in a beautiful setting, and surprisingly, considering it's location, the area is not bothered by smog. It has become the only time each year that I do a race in the LA basin.

That July at Vineman I ended up in the hospital tent again. It seemed that I had become a regular there. As I dragged into the tent one of the nurses recognized me and welcomed me back. At some point during the several hours I was there she commented that I must really love the sport considering what it did to me. Many people may be right to question my sanity, but I do love the sport, and, despite the pitfalls, it has all been worth it to me.

Great North in Davis came around in August again, and this time I won my age group. The main memory of the race concerned the 100+ Canada Geese that lived on the small lake. They were beautiful and great to watch, but their droppings turned the lake water white. Nothing like swimming in diluted goose poop. Oh well, after the porta potties, goose poop is no big deal.

Bass Lake and finally Morro Bay finished out another season, and then it was time to cut back for the winter.

Millerton Lake reappeared on the triathlon scene in 1995 in the form of Mildflower Triathlon, put on by the Fresno State Triathlon Club. The race was held on April 22. The Club put on a good race, however it was not repeated again.

In the early days, many races were sponsored by individuals or clubs. These events were more loosely organized, smaller and cheaper than many races held today. Loosely organized sometimes meant poorly organized, and often equipment was not the best, but at least there was less regimentation and fewer rules. Unfortunately, very few of the more laid back races still exist. The cost in time and effort, along with the modest financial returns have all taken their toll. Older sponsors wear out, younger ones lose interest, and races die. Bass Lake, Castaic, Monterey Bay are some examples of this. The majority of triathlons today are done by professional organizations, and most of these are race series, such as TriCalifornia, J&A, Onyourmark, and Vineman. The events put on by these full time groups are, by and large, great races. They are superbly organized, well equipped, and have adequate volunteers and aid stations. These races are hugely popular, to the point that entries must be made months ahead of time. Camping and parking can be nightmarish, bike courses are sometimes so crowded that crashes become

Larry Owens and Dan Montague at Wildflower

common, and transitions can be many miles apart. I am happy that race sponsors are now able to make a living in the sport and that there is more continuity of races, but something has been lost. Given the economics involved, I don't expect many small races to survive in the future, but it would be nice if there were more of them.

That May at Wildflower, a brand new deraileur broke, and left me sitting beside the road. The Bakersfield and Bonelli races went well. The San Jose Tri was run on the hottest June 25 ever recorded. The Half Vineman was also held on a hot day, but I was able to finish 3rd and didn't get sick until after the race.

The Santa Barbara County Triathlon was held on August 26. I had a terrible allergy attack the afternoon and night before the race, my nose was running like a faucet along with sneezing constantly, and I was unable to sleep most of the night. It was my first time to race in Santa Barbara, and I didn't have a clue about the course, except that we were told to be careful going down Toro Canyon. I had the race of the season. The hills seemed easy, the only time I used my lowest gear was going up the hardest part of Toro Canyon. I'm not a great

64

hill runner, but the run seemed easy, too. The only fatigue I felt was in the last mile of the run on the flat pathway leading to the finish. I finished in second place, 20 seconds behind James Brierton, and later discovered I had spent 30 seconds more in transition than he had. Looking back, that has to be one of the best efforts of my life. I have been back many times and Santa Barbara has become one of my favorite race sites as well as a favorite destination.

That year, the Fresno tri-group put on a great show in Santa Barbara. Nine of us had traveled down there and seven of us came home with awards (tiles). I had ridden down with two friends, John Browning and Jim Harris, both educators, and both fine athletes. The three of us have become friends over the years and often eat together and travel to races as a group. We have all trained until we have nearly worn each other out. Our friendship has added immeasurably to the fun of racing.

Jim Harris at Bass Lake - 1997

I finished the season with third place in Pacific Grove, it's inaugural year, as well as at Bass Lake, and a first in Morro Bay.

10

Training

At this point, it seems appropriate to talk about training. Training is the absolute backbone of triathlon. No matter how suited to endurance athletics your genetic makeup is, you will never succeed in triathlon without adequate and proper training. You or your coach must discover what your strengths and weaknesses are, and train to maximize the former, while minimizing the latter. You must find the point at which your workload limit has been reached. Too little work and you won't perform at your best, too much work and you risk injury and/or illness. To make this puzzle even tougher to figure out, it is necessary to consider your overall fitness at that point, and the time of year you are dealing with. Let me take you through a typical year of my training.

□

The Offseason

For me, the off season begins at the end of the last race of the year, typically near the middle of October. I usually stop biking during this time, runs are reduced to 3-4 miles, 2 to 3 per week, and swims are cut to 2,000 yds, three times weekly. Many years I will hit the road in my camper for 5 or 6 weeks and do only hiking (200 mi approx.) and swim, when a pool is available. To me, this time off is absolutely necessary to repair the wear and tear of a nine month training and racing season. I almost never get through a season without something hurting in October, and it takes time to heal. It is also nice to have a mental break from the regular routine.

Beginning A New Season

Hopefully by January 1, everything feels good again and I'm raring to go. It is important not to try to start where you left off from the previous season. Ease back into it. I increase swimming yardage to 2,500 yds. I begin at 2 mi running and each week increase it a mile up to 4 mi. Biking is done on a wind trainer indoors, and I try to increase the time from a beginning of 30 min, up to 60 min by the end of the month. In February, I try to increase the runs to 6 mi and get in some 25 mi rides. My main goal in February is to be ready for serious training by March.

The Season

In my mind, March is the crux of the whole year. If I have a good training month, I can expect to have a successful year, but inadequate training in March will result in playing catch up all year. My training schedule March through August looks something like this:

	SWIM	BIKE	RUN
Monday	2,500 yards	***	7-10 miles
Tuesday	2,500 yards	50+ miles	***
Wednesday	***	25 miles	4.5 miles
Thursday	2,500 yards	40 high-intensity	***
Friday	Lake Swim (opt.)	50 easy	***
Saturday	2,500 yards	***	6.5 miles
TOTALS:	**10,000 yards**	**150-170 miles**	**17-21 miles**

Wednesday's ride is followed immediately by the run (brick). The high intensity ride is either a hill repeat session or laps around a local park which has some hilly roads. Nearly all of my rides and runs contain hill work. You will note that I train six days a week. I feel strongly that everyone needs to take one day a week as a rest day. I usually take Sunday off to go to church and spend time with my family. If for some reason I'm not able to train on Saturday, then I will do something on Sunday. I am convinced that I am still able to train and race at age 62 because I have given my body one day a week to recuperate.

After August, the long races are over and I feel I can afford to gradually cut back on the training. I cut the rides back to about 30 mi and run no further than 6.5 mi.

Finding time to train adequately is never easy. I have been retired for eight years and it is much easier to get in the miles with no work interference, but for 12 years I fought the same battle every other working person faces. I usually started work at 6AM, and so had time in the afternoons to do most of my training. In all but the shortest days of the winter I could get in a 50 mi ride before dark. By running to the pool, swimming, then running home again, I could log 7 mi running, as well as a swim session, and save the commute time. The same was true of riding to the pool. I was a hospital employee and had to work every third weekend, so I was able to have an occasional day off during the week. These days could be used for long rides. By doing a moderate distance ride, followed by a run (AKA brick) - both at a hard pace, two workouts could be combined into one. I suppose, to sum it up, a person has to just make the time to do the important training needed.

Speaking about importance, triathlon is by no means the most important thing in anyone's life. Family, spouses, children, faith, jobs are all more important than a recreational hobby. Several years ago, over the space of about a year, three of my triathlon friends divorced and their families split up. Training time away from home was not likely the main reason in any of the situations, but it certainly was a factor, and may well have been the straw that broke the camel's back. So be careful to cultivate those relationships needed to sustain a happy life.

Having said all that, let me also say that having an active, athletic lifestyle is very important to me. I really think that training and racing helped me keep my sanity while enduring a thirty year career as a Medical Technologist. Many times I came home from work frustrated and furious, but was able to run it off. I have never gotten out of the pool feeling worse than when I jumped in, and I can usually get rid of a headache just by running or riding. I still weigh 175 lbs, which is what I weighed in college, and I can eat just about anything I want without gaining weight. The hours spent on a long solo bike ride give you time to think about and weigh issues that you face, and time to meditate on the important things in your life.

On the topic of cross training, let me say that while all three of the disciplines help build cardiovascular strength, only biking has much real spillover effect. Swimming and running improve only themselves, but riding does have a beneficial effect on running. Many times because of injury, I have had to cut back or stop running altogether, yet I have been able to race fairly well because of increased riding work. I have tried to ride while doing mainly run training, and it just doesn't work for me. I am long and tall, and tend to over stride while running. I have found that by doing my training rides mostly in the small chain ring and at a high cadence, I am able to keep my running strides shorter and faster, and therefore more efficient.

Preparing For Race Day

After all of the hard training one has already gone through, it is still useful to put the finishing touches on your racing form in the last two weeks leading up to race day. You will want to begin the race fully trained but also well rested. I found through trial and error that beginning ten days before race day I needed to train even harder than usual for a period of six or seven days; sometimes training almost to the point of overtraining. I can tell that I'm nearing overtraining when I feel flu-like symptoms in the evening after the days work is done. I try to push though this routine for a few days. Then starting three full days before the event, I cut back drastically on training; maybe even taking a day off. The other two days are both light days, being sure to do an easy 1000 yd swim session the night before the race, if possible. That evening I always load up on pasta and sauce, if at all possible, to ensure that I have a good glycogen supply the next morning. At least three hours before start time I have a breakfast of either oatmeal or Grape Nuts without any dairy products, a Power Bar, and a banana. Experiment and see what sort of breakfast works for you. I have seen lots of various pre-race meals used by different people which seem to work well for them. Care must be taken not to push yourself too hard during these ten days. You will need to practice and see just how much your body will tolerate before something pops. Remember, there is very little you can do to improve your performance during those last three days and dozens of things that you can do to mess it up. I'll let you make a mental picture of what can go wrong.

The above applies to Olympic or shorter races. If your upcoming race is longer, you will probably need a longer tapering period for your training. For a Half Ironman, 5-7 days will suffice. A Full Ironman distance requires two weeks. Obviously, it is necessary to plan well ahead so you can begin your taper period with the knowledge and confidence that you will be race-ready.

2004 Training Calendar

	RUN (mi)	BIKE (mi)	SWIM (yds)
January	58.5	157	34,450
February	66.5	256	33,050
March	73.5	558	33,700
April	71	503	35,600
May	79	482	32,300
June	41.5	332	29,900
July	42	337	29,500
August	66.5	546	34,200
September	62.5	398	20,600
October	6.5	35	1,900
November	*NO*	*RECORDS*	*THRU*
December	*END*	*OF*	*YEAR*
YEAR TOTAL:	**567.5 mi**	**3,604 mi**	**285,200 yds** (162 miles)
TOTAL SINCE 1989:	**8,652 mi**	**53,906 mi**	**4,133,911 yds** (2,349 miles)

1985 - 2004:
Triathlons: 160 races
Biathlons: 21 races
Adventure: 2 races

11

Socializing

One way to keep training interesting is to make it a social event. For several years on most Friday evenings during the warm months, a group of us would go up to Millerton Lake for an open water swim. After the swim we would light up a barbeque and singe some burgers. The group varied from week to week, but we probably averaged about eight people for several years. We seldom had a master plan, everyone just brought what they wanted and pitched in with the cooking duties. There were several birthday parties, including one for our coach and professional triathlete, John Devere,

The end of a lake swim

which was attended by about 25 people. Some rode bikes to the lake, some did a run, we all ate together and had a good time.

Steve Meunier, Larry Owens, and I had been swimming together for years, and most of the time Larry and I were faster than Steve in the pool, but in races Steve would usually beat both of us out of the water. He probably got more benefit from a wetsuit than Larry or I did, but we accused him of having a pet bass that he would take to races to pull him along while swimming. We were never able to prove the charge but had a lot of fun accusing him of it.

Steve Meunier, Dan Montague, Jim Manfredo

One evening at Millerton Lake, the gang was out in the water doing our usual swim. One of the women, Barbara Anderson, a very attractive redhead, felt something repeatedly bumping her leg. After feeling it several times, she decided one of the guys must be getting fresh and looked up to see who it was. No one was swimming near her; could it have been Meunier's pet bass?

In the last dozen years, several of us have gotten together every Saturday morning for breakfast after swimming. The group has grown, shrunk, and regrown from year to year, and at present we have only about four regulars, but we sit with whoever's there and tell lies and war stories and have a great time.

Barbara Anderson and Dorothy Morse were our social directors for several years, but Barbara moved out of town, and Dot and Larry got married, so the triathlon social scene has died down.

Over the years of racing, I have met many people who live outside the Fresno area whom I would not have gotten to know if not for triathlon. These people have added a lot to the enjoyment of travel and racing, and deserve a place in this story. These are a few of those friends.

Ben Skolnick. Happy Ben! He always has a smile and a good word. I doubt Ben has ever won a race, but he races for the pure love of the sport. I think it speaks well for the quality of triathlon in California that Ben is near the middle of the national rankings for our age group each year.

Joe Russell. At 72, Joe is a consistent age-group winner and is well ranked nationally. He has a well developed sense of humor and is always quick with a good story. Whenever we are at the same race we trade wetsuit zips, I only wish Joe would find a suit with a zipper that is easier to get started. His wife Ruth is equally pleasant and often travels with him to races. They are both fun to be around.

Gerald Gruber is two years younger than me, and a tenacious athlete. We have taken many turns beating each other over the years, although I suspect that he has won more often than I have throughout our personal rivalry. Gerald has fought through some tough physical problems, all the while remaining competitive and cheerful. His wife Mindy usually travels to races with him, and they are always an enjoyable couple to be with.

The Van Horn family from Bakersfield; Jim, the father of the clan; his son Matt; Matt's son, Grant; and Jim's daughter Jennifer and her husband Dwayne. I have had many good times camping near them at Wildflower, and meeting up with them at other races. They are all fine athletes. Grant, at 14, could be a developing star in the sport.

George Nye is another competitor who is faster than I am when he is healthy, but has had injury problems throughout his career. We have pushed each other for years, and have both enjoyed the friendly rivalry.

John Mason is six years my junior, so we never compete head to head when five year age groups are in effect. Nevertheless, neither of us enjoys being beaten by the other, and have kept up a rivalry and friendship for many years. Many times, John has sprinted past me in the last 400 meters of a race, and in the last two years has improved his bike segment to the point that he usually passes me on the ride.

Barbeque lunch following the Bakersfield Triathlon - 1997
From lower left - clockwise: Steve Meunier, John Browning, Faron and Heleen Reed, the author, Jim Harris, Luanna Ottaway, the "unmasked stranger," Ron Ottaway

12

Good Luck, Bad Luck

1996 began in Bakersfield, where I finished second, and where I hurt an ankle on the very rugged course. I wasn't able to run at all through the rest of May and June. In July, I started running a little to try to get ready for Vineman on the 27th. During the race I finished the swim OK, then began the bike segment. At the 20-mile aid station I grabbed a bottle of the sport drink they were using that year, took a swig, and instantly felt nauseated. I managed to get back to the transition area and quit there. I'm sure I was allergic to something in the sport drink. I don't know if the ankle would have held up for 13 miles, but it wasn't tested that day.

Dan Montague at the T2 transition
The Santa Barbara Triathlon - 1996

Steve Meunier at the run
transition in Santa Barbara

In August I tried Santa Barbara, and more bad luck struck. I had a new adjustable aero-bar on my bike, which fell apart a few miles into the race. Every couple of miles another piece fell off and I could hear it clattering on the pavement. Eventually, the aero-bar and attached shifters dropped completely off the handle bars and were hanging down near the brake. On reaching Toro Canyon, I stopped and was able to shift into a low gear, but then

John Browning at Santa Barbara

had to ride back to transition in that low gear. Needless to say, at that point I was hopelessly behind and jogged through the run to an ugly finish time. None of the big guns were in that particular race and I felt as if I had a shot at winning it, so I was really bummed by the result.

The problem-plagued year finished with uninspiring performances at Pacific Grove and Bass Lake. That was one year I could have done without.

The early races of 1997 went satisfactorily, if not great. I placed at Spring Fling, Bakersfield, Wildflower and Bonelli, where I felt I had a very good run. Next came San Jose, where the cards were not in my favor. Robert Plant, Rick Niles, Dennis Honeychurch, Bob Van Vliet, Walter Radloff and Andrew McPherson all beat me even though I did a 2:14 time on the Olympic distance. At that time, I had never beaten any of them, and that day was no different. I had a great race, I just got beaten by some better athletes, no shame in that! In August I finished the Half Vineman and wound up seeing my old friends in the hospital tent again. More IVs. Bless those docs and nurses.

I aged up to 55-59 in mid-August and so went to Santa Barbara in a new age group. Bill Marshall was there, and he is always tough. I was out of the water ahead of him and stayed there until about three miles before the transition, where he passed me. I figured that was that. However, about four miles into the run I saw him ahead of me, moving slowly. Suddenly, he stepped off the course and into a clump of bushes. I saw my chance and took it. I got ahead of him without his knowledge. He finally saw me near the turnaround. I was in the lead and had to push hard to stay there. I kept ahead of Bill until mile eight, when nausea forced me to pull off and heave awhile. He passed me, and went on to finish a with a win. I was second, and won my only trip ever to the hospital tent at Santa Barbara. The view of the beach and ocean is better in Santa Barbara, but the nurses are better looking at Vineman.

In September, Dave Moon beat me by 20 seconds at Great North, I finished third at Pacific Grove, and placed second at Bass Lake.

The *Fossils and Fuzz* team at the Sierra Challenge Adventure Race - 1997
Dan Montague, Larry Owens, Dot Morse, Steve Meunier, John Browning

On September 27-28, I teamed with John Browning, Steve Meunier, and Larry Owens to do the Sierra Challenge Adventure Race. We called our team "Fossils and Fuzz" - John, Larry, and I were the fossils, and Steve, a Deputy Sheriff, was the fuzz. The course began at 6AM, with a five mile run, then a 16 mile canoe, a 64 mile road bike into the Sierra's, a 20 mile hike, a 45 mile mountain bike and a five mile run to the finish. Eight teams were entered and each team had a sag wagon and driver to transport gear from one transition to the next. The idea of the run at the start was to spread the teams out, but no team pushed the pace, so we all started the canoe in one big group. White water and inexperience soon spread things out. Several canoes capsized and one was wrecked, but no one was hurt.

The 64 mi bike course climbed up more than 7,000 ft and was done during the hottest part of the 95 degree day. Several teams had come from the cooler coastal areas of the state to participate in the event, and since they weren't used to the high temperatures, the heat really hit them hard. Two of the teams had dropped out by the end of the ride. By the time *Fossils and Fuzz* reached the trailhead at 7,500 ft, it was nearly dark. Our sag wagon driver Dot Owens had a supper of spaghetti and french bread ready for us when we arrived. Once we were refueled, we put on our packs and head lamps and headed into the woods. We walked until midnight, then stopped for three hours to catch up on some sleep. Once refreshed, we pressed on and

The author and John Browning in the canoe leg of the race

crossed the 10,000 ft pass just before dawn. Our team reached the next transition area about 10AM, and again, Dot was waiting for us with a hot meal.

At this point, another group dropped out. They had spent most of the night lost in the forest and were no longer speaking to each other. Once again fueled up, it was time for us *Fossils* to start the 45 mi mountain biking segment. The course went down, down, down, ... 8,000 ft down. Near the finish, the temperature was again 95 degrees. We had experienced 95 at the beginning of the race, then

Running 5
Cycling 70
Canoeing 15
Hiking 20
Mountain Biking 45
Running 5

Sierra Challenge event jacket

freezing atop the pass, then 95 again. Browning commented that it felt like he had "died and gone to Hell." It was quite a temperature range to go through in a 24 hour period. There was one more transition, followed by a five mile run - then we were done!

The *Fossils and Fuzz* finished about 3PM for a total time of 33 hours, and third place overall. Five teams finished, although only three had all members complete the entire distance. Lots of food awaited us at the finish, but most of us were too tired to eat. Finishing that race was one of the most satisfying things I have done, second only to the Aconcagua summit.

Although completely exhausted, I raced twice more in October. Winning in Morro Bay, and having a terrible race at Gateway To Yosemite, but still came in second.

13

If It Weren't For Bad Luck,
I'd Have No Luck At All

Despite some setbacks, 1997 had been a great year. I had done thirteen races, placing in all but two, and had also completed an adventure race.

Following the fine season I had in 1997, I was expecting 1998 to be at least as good. My first full year in the 50-54 age group had been my best ever, and I was hoping for the same in my first 55-59 year - I was in for a real disappointment. Things began well enough with a 2nd place at Spring Fling and also at Wildflower, and a personal record and 3rd at Bonelli. Two months later was the Full Vineman big race, for which I had trained very hard. I focused especially on my riding, putting in many days of 80, 90 and 100 miles, and was in the best long race condition of my life on race day. Things went well enough through the first fifty miles on the bike. I had been asking for and drinking only water, remembering the problem I had with the sport drink. At the fifty mile aid station I asked for water and a powerbar. The person passing out liquids gave me the dreaded sport drink by accident, and I put it in the bottle rack, grabbed a bar, and immediately ate it. After eating the bar, I needed to wash it down and so reached for the bottle. I immediately knew what was wrong, but was so dry that I swallowed the sport drink anyway. Instant nausea again! I pushed on for another 30 miles, but was forced to stop near Jimtown. I barfed up everything but my toenails, and won another ride in a sagwagon to the hospital tent. There, I was received like an old friend and treated royally, as always. I was really bummed to be out of the race for such a stupid reason. I had trained

Out of the water - Santa Barbara, 1998

harder than ever, and believed I had learned enough about hydrating and pacing to survive to the finish, but no such luck.

Santa Barbara was next, and I had to retire from the race because of a flat tire on the bike. This was followed by an average performance in Pacific Grove. Bass Lake came next, and was an absolute disaster. During the swim, a low cloud moved in making visability almost zero. Bass Lake is only about 200 yards wide at that point, and I would have never believed it was possible to get lost in a lake so narrow, but let me assure you, it is possible. With no shoreline in sight, it was impossible to navigate, and it was impossible to find the finish chute. A group of about forty of us were milling around together out there in the water. Someone would say, "This way" - and we would all swim in that direction, to no avail. Then someone else would say "That way" - which didn't work either. Finally, John Devere, who was supervising the swim heard us yelling, and yelled back telling us to follow the sound of his voice and he would lead us to the finish. Normally it takes me about 27 minutes to do that swim, but that day I was in the water for almost an hour. While swimming, I failed to notice that the rain had started to fall heavily, and it continued all through the bike ride. The temperature must have been in the forties, and along with being soaking wet, I was so cold I couldn't feel my hands on the brakes. The hands still worked, but I had to look down to see if they were on the brake levers whenever I needed to slow down. After the bike, the run was a piece of cake. It was possible to stay warm while running. Many people abandoned the race after the swim, but some of us held out to the frigid end.

For my last performance of the year, I traveled to Morro Bay. John Browning owns a house in Cayucos where I often stay when we are racing in the area, and I had spent the night with him and his wife. The race application had stated that there would be no race day entries, but I thought they would relent, as I knew they had only 60 entries. I drew a hard-nosed volunteer at the registration desk, and she wouldn't let me enter, even though I had won my age group the year before. The perfect ending to an awful year.

The awful year carried over into 1999. Bakersfield was my first race. I was the only 55-59 entered, and so therefore won by default. It was at this race that the "gel and no water" incident occurred. I was the only person from Fresno there and I was too sick to go to the award ceremony, so I didn't get the trophy. I lay in my camper all afternoon spitting up glops of undigested gel. Not until the next morning was I able to keep anything down. The next race was at Bonelli, and on the second lap of the bike I lost control on a slick spot rounding a turn and crashed the bike. I got up, decided that nothing worse than road rash had happened and got back on the bike only to find that a tire had blown - race over. Next came San Jose. The lucky streak continued. This time it was

John Browning and the author, Santa Barbara winners - 1999

a flat which I was unable to fix. Then it was Vineman. Sick again - out again.

Browning down the final hill at Bakersfield

It was time for some personal reassesment. I decided I had two options. First, I could quit and crawl off into a hole somewhere and feel sorry for myself. Second, I could go on, work even harder, and try to make a success of the rest of the season. The second idea seemed to be the better of the two.

I had a month of training time before Santa Barbara, and I used it well. For a change, nothing went wrong and I finished third. This was followed by another third in Pacific Grove, and a second at Angel's Camp. Whether it was pure chance or bad attitude or a combination of the two, I can't say, but things turned around and what had been a disasterous season ended on a positive note.

In 2000, a major change took place at Bakersfield. For years, the race had been a standard Olympic distance, with a 6 mile run. The application form listed the run distance as 9 miles, but I thought it must be a typo and trained for a 6 mile. I was painfully surprised when I found the error was mine and not the forms. There was nothing to do but go for it. I managed to win the age group in spite of myself. I also found that I liked the new distance. The Bakersfield run course is sandy in places, steep and rutted and rocky in others; it's a real challenge and very satisfying to finish. It is a great race and a great course, and I look forward to it each year.

Wildflower was a good race and party, as always, and it was even more crowded than ever. I managed a third in the Olympic distance.

The Millerton Lake Triathlon was resurrected in 2000 by Faron and Heleen Reed under their Sierra Multisports Productions organization. It was a new course on the north side of the lake and turned out to be both difficult and interesting, with lots of hills on both the bike and run segments, and cold water in the lake. I'm not a strong hill runner, but managed a race I was pleased with. All of us locals were happy to see this new encarnation of the race. At Bonelli, I finally won my age group for the first time on that course. This was followed by good efforts at San Jose and San Luis Obispo.

Santa Barbara was noteworthy to me because I finally managed to finish ahead of Ian Reed. Ian and I had been racing at about the same level for years. I was better in the swim, we were fairly evenly matched on the bike and he was much better on the run. I had calculated that on that course I needed a 10 minute lead going into the run to have a chance to beat him, and It is not easy to build up a 10 minute lead on a good athlete. I didn't see Ian until after the

Three "OLD" Winners - Angel's Camp, 2000
Chris Denny (60-69), Dan Montague (50-59), Chuck Freuler (70-79)

turnaround on the run and could see that my lead was good enough to hold up. I pushed as hard as I could and beat him by four minutes. I ended up with fourth place and a tile. Another happy trip to Santa Barbara.

I always look forward to Pacific Grove for two reasons. The most important one is that I have an opportunity to see my Aunt Ada, who lives 300 yards from Lover's Point. Ada is one of my favorite people in the whole world, and the chance to get together with her, and do a good race, is just too good to pass up. John Browning and I go every year, and Ada always treats John like one of the family. Anyway, after climbing over the kelp, and wandering through the fog on the bike, I started the run a minute behind Phillip Darst and a little ahead of Ian Reed. I caught Darst near the turnaround on the third lap and held off Reed, and thought I had the win, only to find later that I had been nailed with the only drafting penalty I've gotten in 160 races. The two minute penalty dropped me to third.

A win at Angel's Camp and another at Merced's Gateway to Yosemite, finished a very satisfying season. A season very much better than the previous two. The decision a year earlier to work harder and stick with the sport turned out to be the right one.

My triathlon career has a lot in common with a roller coaster ride. 1999 and 2000 had both ended as good years, so I guess I was due for a fall. The early training in 2001 progressed well enough and I was ready to race at Spring Fling in early April. I finished second and was satisfied with that. It has seemed that over the years, I need a race like Spring Fling, something low key, to really get me ready to push hard on the bike. Training alone doesn't prepare me for the intensity of racing as well as an early, short race.

Millerton Lake was two weeks later, and fell on one of the coldest, wettest, and windiest weekends we have had for years. I drove up in my camper before the race to help Faron Reed set up the transition area, then stayed the night. Not long after dark, a hard wind blew up and dropped the temperature dramatically, which was then followed by rain and hail. It rained much of the night, but cleared by dawn.

When I looked outside the camper, snow was visable on the hilltops not far from the lake. A very cold wind was still blowing; not ideal for a race. The lake water wasn't too bad during the swim, but the cold air made the ride miserable. It is a hard, hilly ride under any circumstances, but the wind made it much worse. The run is also tough, a hilly trail run, but at least keeping warm was easier. I took first in the 50-59 and was happy with my performance. Coming off the bike, my feet were numb, and only after a mile of running was I able to feel my feet hitting the ground. Somewhere during the run I injured my left foot, and it bothered me all the rest of the season.

On May 6 At Wildflower, my foot was still painful, but I was still able to race and finish fourth, 25 seconds behind Jim Orear. I had run close behind him for most of the six miles and could see that he was hurting and could be beaten, but I was too tired myself to make a move. After the race, my foot was almost to sore to walk on. The next week I saw my podiatrist and asked him to reline my orthotics. That helped, but the problem persisted. I did Bonelli again in June, and had a good effort and a third place finish, but the foot was so painful that John Browning had to do all the driving going home.

The *Phillips Four* at Santa Barbara with their four awards - 2001; Anne, Jenny, Jeff, Pat

Early that summer I was training on my bike in the foothills some 20 miles east of Fresno, and stopped for lunch at a favorite Mexican restaurant in the town of Prather. This was during one of my recurrent bouts of foot problems; my left foot was so painful that I could hardly flex it. After finishing lunch I was heading back towards the highway when I noticed a group of young women standing with their bicycles along the roadside. I thought it would be cool to ride past them and say 'Hi' to some fellow bikers. As I neared, I apparently was paying more attention to the girls than oncoming traffic, and failed to notice cars coming from both directions. I had nowhere to go and no choice but to brake hard. I tried to get my left foot out of the pedal binding, but couldn't because of the soreness. I then tried to release the right foot, but by that time it was too late and I began to fall, landing right in front of the ladies. To make the scene even worse, I still couldn't get loose from the pedals, so I laid on the road for several seconds struggling to get free of the bike. Eventually I escaped, and nothing more than my pride was injured. The girls wanted to know if I was OK; I was too embarrassed to explain what had happened. Even veteran bikers mess up sometimes.

Later in June, I traveled to Indonesia for my niece Holly's wedding. Several of the family traveled together and we had a great time at the wedding, after which, we toured Java and Bali for ten days. The countryside is lush and green and beautiful, and the Indonesian people were kind and gracious. I felt no anti-American antagonism at all, and things went very well except for the nasty virus I picked up somewhere. It began with vomiting and progressed to "the trots." The phrase "eat and run" took on a whole new meaning! The problem was still with me a month after returning home and I finally saw my doctor. Diagnosis: colitis; treatment: enemas -'nuff said.

In October, I left in my camper for ten weeks of travel and hiking in the canyon country of Utah, New Mexico, and Arizona. What a wonderful way to regain one's strength and see some of the most beautiful country on the planet. I hiked 335 miles during the ten weeks, and saw Bandelier, Capital Reef, Mesa Verde, Grand Canyon, and many other great spots, and came home just in time for Christmas, once again healthy and fit.

14

Things Look Up

In April of 2002, several of us entered the Palm Springs Triathlon. We arrived at the Cahuilla Lake race site after dark, and so were unable to survey the course. In the morning we discovered that the lake was completely dry. A canal had broken a few days earlier, and to keep irrigation water running to the local farms, the lake had been drained. It's hard to do a swim in a dry lake, so race management changed it into a run-bike-run format. I had a flat during the bike and didn't finish. The other three Fresnans all brought home medals.

At Bakersfield I did something I had never, ever, expected to do. I finished ahead of Walter Radloff. I had beaten him out of the water, only to have him pass me on the bike. He was a little ahead of me at the start of the run, but still within sight. I stopped for a minute and he was gone when I stepped back on the course. I thought, "Well, that's the last I'll see of him today." After about three miles on the first long gradual hill, I looked up and there he was, moving slowly and apparently hurting. I soon passed him, and as I went by, commented, "I never thought I'd get to do this!" After the race, he came up and congratulated me, which I thought was a gracious thing for him to do. As I said before, I have known Walter a long time, and have always enjoyed yakking with him at races. He is a knowledgeable, talkative person, and always interesting. His performance had been so much better than mine for so long that I really never expected to beat him.

By the time I attempted to register for San Jose in June, the Olympic race was sold out, so I entered the Mt. Bike race. I don't really like riding a Mt. Bike and don't like trail racing at all, but I did it anyway, and won the 55-59 division. It was a new experience, one which I haven't repeated, but at least I completed one Mt. Bike race.

2002 was the inaugural year for J&A's Folsom Triathlon. The water was achingly cold, the bike easy, and the run was all uphill on the way out, and all downhill coming back. I was third at the finish, with Robert Plant winning. Folsom is a good venue for a race, and was even better in 2003 since the transition area was moved a few miles down the American River.

In mid-August I aged up into 60-64, just in time for Santa Barbara. The race is usually dominated by Vic Bertalan, but he is a few months younger than me, so I have one race every five years in which I don't have to compete with him. I took advantage of the chance and took home my first 1st Place Tile. The tiles given as awards are unique to that race and make an interesting collection. The win completed my set of 1st through 4th.

The author with the First Place award
Santa Barbara - 2002

I raced three more times that fall and won all of the events: Pacific Grove Sprint, Angel's Camp, and Merced's Gateway to Yosemite. That gave me four wins in my first four races in the new age group. Winning is usually a little easier soon after you age up; you compete against older men, and escape your younger rivals for a little while.

15

Food

Food and eating are something triathletes are famous for. Most of us burn huge numbers of calories in our training and can eat almost anything we want without gaining weight. It is wonderful to be able to dig into a mountain of spaghetti without guilt. At times, my training schedule leaves me exhausted and worn out. I have found that a really large pasta dinner will usually have me fixed up and ready to go the next morning. Other than that, I don't seem to feel any different, no matter what I eat.

I watch my salt and fat intake for general health purposes, and have lots of fruit and some veggies, but other than that, I don't worry too much about what's on my plate. I sometimes forget that not all bodies function alike. I was spouting off one time in a group, saying that if anyone trained enough, he could eat anything he wanted. A friend responded that he had once run 60 miles per week and still gained weight. That threw me for a loop, and forced me to re-evaluate my views. I still maintain that most people will lose weight if they eat a moderate, balanced diet and exercise moderately. By moderately I don't mean they need to train like I do. I likely train at least twice as much as is needed for health and fitness. I train to be competitive, and that is far beyond what the average person needs to do.

Food is a large part of most peoples social life, and I think even more so for the triathlete. As I have said, the Fresno triathlete group eats together at least once a week on Saturday morning after swimming. I also eat often with John Browning and his family, as well as with Jim Harris and his wife. Eating with friends is a great addition to my life and I hope to their's, as well.

I plan most of my long rides so that twelve-noon and the Dam Diner in Friant coincide. They serve great burgers and other dishes in huge portions. It really isn't my fault that I always stop there, my bike just turns into their parking lot automatically - not my fault at all. From time to time, Jim Harris rides with me and we eat there, and occasionally we are joined by my cousin, Joe Montague. The waitresses know me well enough that almost as soon as I sit down, an icy cold coke appears on the table. They remember from year to year not to put salt on the fries and that I usually order the "Western Burger."

I don't usually snack much during a ride. If I'm doing 50 or more miles, I do usually stop at about halfway and have a Powerbar and water. As I have stated, I take a gel at the start of the run in a race, and if it is longer than six miles another gel about halfway through.

As you can see, my major concern about food is only that there be plenty of it. I know many will not agree with this approach, but it has worked for me. I learned to eat this way from my parents. They ate what was available, enjoyed it, and didn't really give it a second thought. Both of my parents lived to be active into their late eighties, and died at ages 89 and 92. I hope to do as well.

16

Let The Good Times Roll

In early April, John Browning, Chuck Freuler, Walt Brown and I went to Palm Springs, again for their sprint distance race. This time there was plenty of water in Lake Cahuilla, and everything went as planned. I was outsprinted by Steve Schumacher for third place and finished out of the money, for what turned out to be the only time that year. At Millerton Lake I was beaten by John Mason, and was second in the 50 and up age group.

Next came Wildflower. Robert Plant usually dominates this race, but he aged up just after Wildflower, and so I thought I had a good shot at my first win in that race. The only known threat on the entry list was Jack Sorenson and he didn't show up. I thought I had it made. It is said that pride goes before the fall and I made several poor decisions and was beaten by Vern Holthouse. I had blown my one real chance to win the race, a chance that comes only once in five years.

Friday night, the night before the long course, it rained nearly three inches and turned the whole area into a muddy quagmire. At start time it was still raining lightly, on and off, and was cold. For five minutes the swimmers in transition would be in sunshine, and would head out onto the bike in their shorts and tops. Then for five minutes it would rain again, and the next batch of riders would leave wearing rain gear. Part of the run was on trail that was impassable, and was therefore re-routed so that everything was on pavement. The campground became a soggy mess with a small creek flowing through it. Many entries saw the situation and went home. It could have been a complete washout, so to speak, but the TriCalifornia team did a great job of adapting to a bad situation and still produced a good race. People in the mountain bike race were faced with lots of deep mud and terrible going, but most got through it all, even if they did look more like mud babies than people at the finish.

Bakersfield age-group winners - 2003
Chuck Freuler, John Browning,
Dan Montague

Conditions on Sunday were much improved, although it was necessary to reroute the run again to avoid the muddy dirt roads. We rode on dry pavement and were blessed with some sunshine. On the following weekend I raced at Bakersfield and won 60-64 in spite of a painful foot, and a week later I placed third behind Robert Plant, now aged up, and Bill Marshall at Uvas.

Friends had been telling me to do the Uvas race for several years, but for various reasons I just hadn't done it. I'm sorry it took so long. It is a good, short race in a beautiful area. I was shocked to find anything that pretty near San Jose. The ridges are very rugged and green, the housing is new and expensive; it is a great venue for a race. I plan to compete there again.

June 1 found Jim Harris and me at Bonelli. As always, it was a fun race. The lake was murky, and the air was clear. It was Jim's first experience down there and he liked it well enough to go back. I felt I had a mediocre race, but it was good enough to win. As Walter Radloff once said, "A win is a win." I beat Steve Schumacher by nearly four minutes and so avenged the loss to him at Palm Springs. Jim took second.

95

Three weeks later, Browning and I were back at San Jose. He for the short course on Saturday and me for the Olympic distance on Sunday. We both usually place well in our races and this was no exception. John won, and I was second to Robert Plant.

Following San Jose, I had a five week break between races, and used the time to take a trip to Iceland with Steve Meunier and Jim Goold, a friend from the pool. We did the touristy stuff in Reykjavic, took a ferry to the Arctic Circle at Grímsey Island off the northern coast of the country, and finished the trip with a three day hike in the wildlife refuge at Hornvík in the Westfjords of northwest Iceland. During the hike we managed to lose the trail in fog, spend a damp

Iceland, 2003 - Arctic Circle marker on Grímsey Island: 66°33' N latitude
Dan Montague, Steve Meunier, Jim Goold

night in the tent, and hike most of the next day in pouring rain. It was cold and miserable, and a great experience. The six hour Arctic Ocean boat ride from Hornvík Bay back to civilization was so rough that some of the Vikings on board got sea sick. We land-lubber Americans somehow got through it unscathed.

After returning home from Iceland, my next race was the non-competitive San Luis Obispo, always a fun outing in a great race area. Jim Harris, Browning, his daughter Shannon and I all did the race. There are no awards, just a finisher's medal. It is primarily geared for beginners and kids, but it is fun for all who participate.

Folsom, with it's new and much improved course, was held on August 10. Again, Browning and I traveled together, he for the short course and I for the Olympic race. We both won our respective age groups. The win gave me a first, a second, and a third for the year in J&A races. The new venue provided much better parking, warmer water, and a more interesting run than the first year's race. Also, the layout of the course is such that spectators can view much of the run from the transition area.

At Santa Barabara, Vic Bertalan had aged up, Bill Marshall showed up, and some "joe blow" came out of nowhere and I wound up placing fourth. My time was eight minutes slower than my winning time the year before, but if I had finished eight minutes faster I still would have come in fourth.

After Santa Barbara, I was back again at Pacific Grove and Aunt Ada's house. I was second to Elias Olson by nearly three and a half minutes, and one minute ahead of George Nye. I haven't raced against Olson much, but he has always beaten me.

I finished the year with wins in Angel's Camp, Shaver Lake (a new race put on by Sierra Multisport Productions), and Gateway to Yosemite in Merced. It turned out to be my best season ever, with six wins: 4 seconds, 1 third, and 1 fourth.

When I started this tale, I expected to be finished months ago. It turned out that I was overly optimistic, and now have had time to write about the 2004 season, as well as the previous 19 campaigns. This enabled me to include "20 Years of Tri-ing" in the book title.

The first race of the year was the Spring Fling on March 27, which was put on locally by Sierra Multisports. It was not technically a triathlon but a run-bike-run, or duathlon. I have always used this early season event as a fitness check, as well as an opportunity

Holly Chohan in the bike transition
at Spring Fling

to get my legs used to pushing at race pace for the Triathlons to come. I was especially looking forward to this event because my niece Holly Chohan was doing her first ever race. I had been picking at her since she was three years old to become a triathlete, never remotely thinking she would ever want to. I was pleasantly surprised when she announced her intention. She had been training over the winter and was well prepared for a first event. She even had her own cheering section of nine people there to root her on. Actually, I'm jealous. I can think of only six people who have come to see me race in 20 years, and here she draws nine for her first race. Oh well, she is much better looking than I am.

Spring Fling is a small local race. I was the only 60+ male entered, and so won by default. Holly surprised herself, (although I wasn't surprised) and came in third in her age group. After the race, Holly and I, along with her entourage, went out to the Dam Diner to celebrate. Nothing like a good hearty meal after a race to get you ready for more training.

The Bakersfield Triathlon was contested on April 17, and turned out
to be a cool day - ideal for distance racing. The course was rugged
as always, and a real challenge. I always enjoy the run course with
it's sand, hills and rocks. When you finish, you know you have done
something substantial. Once again, I was the only one in the 60-64
age group and an automatic winner. Although winning by default is
of itself meaningless, I had a respectable time and was satisfied with
the effort. As Walter Radloff said, "A win is a win, take it. Everyone
else could have raced and chose not to."

South Bay at Uvas Reservoir, in the hills south of San Jose, was held
on April 25. In 2003, Robert Plant had won first, Bill Marshall was
second, with me coming in third. This year, George Nye was there,
healthy after several years of nagging injuries. I had usually been
able to beat George while he was hurt, but now found what a good
athlete he is when he is healthy. Plant and Marshall were first and
second again with Nye finishing two minutes ahead of me, again in
third. I stayed ahead of George through the bike only to have him
transition faster and get a lead I wasn't able to make up during the
run. It isn't ever fun to be fourth in a race, but if you take the wins,
you better be able to take the losses. Uvas is a great early season
race. The hills and lake are beautiful, J&A does a wonderful job
staging the event, and it seems to attract a strong field each year.

Next came the "Woodstock of Triathlon" - Wildflower, held on
May 1 & 2. The 2003 race was in pouring rain and winter-like cold.
Conditions in 2004 could not have been more different. Both days
were well over 100 degrees, making racing miserable and dangerous.
Hundreds of people were treated in the hospital tent for heat related
problems over the two days. In spite of the heat it was a great
weekend, meeting old friends, making new friends, watching a race
one day, racing yourself another day. The TriCalifornia organization
always puts on a memorable event on the best triathlon course
in California. It is crowded, hectic, awesome and, above all, fun.
There is an energy pervading the whole event that I have never
experienced anywhere else; a tension of built up energy waiting to be

released out on the race course in competition. It is a beautiful thing to see and feel!

I did the Olympic distance again this year. The competition was George Nye, Thomas Duket, me, Phillip Darst, and Vern Holthouse, in the order we finished. Nye passed me on the bike, I passed Darst four miles onto the run and was 20 seconds behind Duket at the finish. Somewhere during the long hill coming out of Harris Creek I pulled up with a cramping hamstring and was given a salt tablet by John Campbell, who saw what was happening and stopped to help. It was a very nice gesture and I appreciated it a lot. I was then able to finish the run in good form.

I had taken more water than usual during the race, due to the heat, but it was not enough. I could tell at the finish I would likely be sick and went down to the lake to try to cool off in the water. It was just too hot. I went to the hospital tent along with a mass of other people, and was taken in and treated very well as I mentioned earlier in the book. After receiving two liters of IV fluid, I was released and went to the shady area near the stage. I was still there when they called my name in third place during the awards ceremony, but was afraid I would throw up in front of everyone if I went up. I just sat there quietly. The medal was later sent to me.

My only race in June this year was the San Jose International Triathlon on the 13th. John Browning and I drove up on Friday, he raced the mountain bike race on Saturday the 12th, and my race was the next day. It is fun to travel with someone as easy to get along with as Browning, always good natured and witty. I have met a lot of new people because of him. He easily makes conversation with anyone around, and I'm usually able to join in. If I am by myself, I am generally quiet and don't often start conversations. I have to say, it is nice to have someone to trade off driving with on the way home after a hard race. Often, I tell John that he is doing the wimp race and he counters by saying that he is the smart, good looking one of the group. During his race I usually yell, "Hey Browning - go, you old buzzard!" The old buzzard usually wins his race, which is more than I can say. I finished third behind Robert Plant and Bill Marshall. My time was 2:31:23, an effort I was happy with. Over the last three years I have noticed my times have dropped off two to three minutes per year for any given race. San Jose was no exception. I hear other age groupers saying the same thing, so at least I'm not alone. At some point, one must be happy just being able to keep racing at a competitive level.

The San Luis Obispo Triathlon was my only race in July. It is a non-competitive race with no awards and is mostly about promoting fitness. Nonetheless, some real jocks enter and it is a fun event with no pressure. My niece Holly entered, and did her first swim event as part of the race. She was nervous before the start, but got through the swim, then biked and ran well. She didn't finish third in her age group, but was happy to have completed the course. I am very proud of her for putting in the time and effort to learn the skills and achieve the fitness necessary to race in triathlon.

That August I did two races. The first was Folsom International, a fast, relatively easy course along the American River, east of Sacramento. I was second this time, beaten by George Nye again. The second race was Santa Barbara. I had my best race of the year, but still finished out of the money. Vic Bertalan was the winner, followed by Elias Olson, Carl Cuhn, and Bill King for the four podium spots, with me coming in fifth. Considering the quality of the men who beat me, I felt gratified to have competed well against them. I felt like I had put all I had out on the course and that is all I expect of myself.

On September 11, it was time to do the *Kelp Crawl with the Great Whites* at Pacific Grove. As well as being the tenth annual P.G. Triathlon it was the third anniversary of the 9-11 attack, so there was a memorial ceremony before the race start. Each athlete left a US flag bearing the name of a 9-11 victim sticking in the sand near the start area, and each of us had the same name taped to our bike helmet during the bicycle portion of the race.

We old buzzards (45+) started as the fifth wave, and by that time, the kelp had been worn down somewhat and was not as much a problem as it usually is, so the swim went well although the water was 55 degrees. The day was misty and I had problems with foggy glasses all during the ride. I could barely see the road, but got through the 25 miles without incident. I knew I was ahead of Elias Olson and had passed Phillip Darst at about 10 miles into the bike, so I figured I was leading for most of the bike. Olson passed me just as we were pulling into the run transition, then built on his lead to best me by four minutes at the finish. Ian Reid had also passed Darst to place third.

One week later on September 18, I was at Angel's Camp for Onyourmark's tough, short-course triathlon. It was a cool, overcast day, perfect for racing. The lake level was very low, so we had a l-o-n-g climb to the transition area, a hilly bike, then a hilly run to the finish. I won the 60+ age group, and actually had competition this time, so the win really meant something.

The Shaver Lake Triathlon was held on September 25. I had not done the Olympic distance race there, and soon discovered that it was a very tough course. The elevation is 5300 ft, the thinner air is definitely noticeable. The bike course is all hills with one long gradual climb and lots of rollers, so the out is mostly hard climbing and the back mostly fast downhill. The run was two loops of hills, with the first mile of each loop on a trail through the forest and the last two miles on pavement. It was a fun, tough race which I again won by default. This is a race which is worth doing if you are looking for a late season race in a beautiful area.

Onyourmark's Gateway to Yosemite in Merced, held on October 3, was my last race of the year. I can't explain what happened, but my time of 2:16:30 was nine minutes faster than last year's time on the same course. Most races I have done this year have been slower than last years. Go figure! I won and beat the second place finisher by nearly 45 minutes. It was a great way to finish a satisfying season, and the end of my first twenty years in triathlon.

17

Misadventures

I have mentioned road rash and a broken collar bone, but there are other injuries that bedevil triathletes, as well. When a rider crashes, the hardest impact is usually to the hip. Both Ron Ottaway and Brian Fehrenbach sustained hip injuries that put them out of action for the remainder of the season. Several local triathletes have crashed and hit their heads, but have been saved by their helmets. Steve Meunier, Jim Manfredo, Larry Owens, and Faron Reed have all undergone knee surgeries to repair damaged cartlidge. Meunier, John Browning and Darrel Hale have all had severe back problems which were not caused by racing, but were certainly made worse by it. Anne Phillips suffered from Chronic Fatigue Syndrome which was likely due in part to heavy training, while also being a wife, mother, dental technician, as well as a triathlete. I have had chronic achilles and foot/ankle problems most of my career, but fortunately nothing that needed surgery. Larry Owens has had a series of muscle and joint problems that have forced him to cut back his training drastically and forced him to stop racing entirely.

To non athletes it must sound like we are all either masochists or just plain crazy - I suggest that is not the case. We all have adopted a healthy lifestyle which we love a lot and which gives us great satisfaction, in spite of the difficulties. It is also a social outlet with like-minded people, which I think has added a lot to all our lives. I have never heard anyone state that he or she was sorry to have gotten involved in triathlon.

I have mentioned sore feet and ankles many times. In March 2003, I finally discovered what was causing the problem. The pain was usually less in the off-season, but always seemed to return every spring. As I increased my running mileage in the spring, the foot began hurting again. One day as I was looking at the step-in cleats on my bike shoes, I realized that they were set so that I was riding with a constant twist on the ankle. My theory as to how this happened is that each time I replaced the cleats, I outlined it with a pencil so as to put the new one in the same position. I must have fudged the right cleat slightly to the inside each time, and eventually got it so far out of line that there was constant tension on that ankle. I then set the cleats in a neutral position and the pain lessened immediately. Improvement continued throughout the year, and by fall I was running with little pain. This year (2004) I have been able to run without soreness for the first time in several years. Sometimes a little mistake can cause major problems. It pays to think about everything you do and the consequences of that action.

Many things can happen to any athlete who uses the roads and waterways for training. Open-water swims put a swimmer at risk from high-speed boats and marine life, runners must watch out for traffic and weather, but most of the problems a triathlete encounters happen while biking. Some people don't think we have any right to share their roads, and many drivers don't watch the road as they should. Some see sport in harassing bikers, and others have been mistreated themselves by errant riders, and so have a deserved grudge against cyclists.

I have logged over 50,000 miles on the bicycle and so have spent a lot of time out on the road and in harms way. During that time, I have had firecrackers thrown at me twice, several water bottles, cups of soda with ice, and an empty wine bottle. Teenage boys seem to get a special thrill from screaming out of an open car window just as they pull even with a rider. Sometimes it is only a scream, sometimes it is personal. People noises don't bother me much, but a dog in the back of a pick-up truck, barking in my ear as he goes by always makes me jump. Then there was the topless young lady leaning out a car window to wave at me. I guess I must admit, that was more a distraction than a bother.

The wine bottle incident involved a pickup-load of teen age boys apparently coming home from the lake after a party. As they passed, someone threw a bottle in front of my bike expecting me to run through the broken glass. Fortunately for me, the pavement widened a bit at that spot and they had misjudged the distance enough that I was able to swing around the glass. Two more riders were a quarter mile ahead of me and the same thing happened to them. I am always so surprised when something like that happens that I never think to get a license plate number.

Once, while on a long ride through the hills above Fresno, John Browning and I were riding and talking as we rode two abreast over a small hill. A car came up behind us faster than he should have been going on the one lane road, and had to break to avoid us. He then passed with his horn blasting and obviously swearing at us. I stupidly shook my fist at him, whereupon he slammed on the brakes and jumped out. He was at least 6'3" and built like a linebacker. Right then and there I knew I had made a big mistake. I don't think he really wanted to fight any more than I did, but he screamed in my face for a couple minutes. Fortunately, I did nothing to provoke him further, and he drove on.

The moral to this story is that as a biker, you can never win in these situations. A car is heavier, faster, and bigger than you are. You can never tell who is in that car and what he may bring to a confrontation. The best way to react is to not react at all. Swallow your anger and pride and live to ride another day.

I am by no means the only person to have been assaulted on the road. John Devere had a handful of pennies thrown at him and was hit by several of them. It was painful, but fortunately no serious damage was done. On another occasion, a large metal spoon was thrown at him - it missed. Steve Meunier, Deputy Sheriff, was riding in the hills near his home one day, when a high school student screamed in his ear, "Get that f----- bike off the road!" Steve recognized the kid and knew where he was going. He followed behind the car, and sure enough, it was parked at a local mini mart, just where he thought it would be. Steve went in and had a heart to heart chat with that young man. When confronted by the Law, the kid was heavy on the "Yes, sirs" and the "I'm sorrys."

I don't mean to imply that bikers are never in the wrong. The incident with the linebacker would not have happened if we had been riding in single file, or if I hadn't made the gesture. I have seen groups of riders who were riding several abreast refuse to get out of the way when honked at. I have seen riders cut in front of cars that had the right of way, and other times I have heard riders curse drivers and make unpleasant hand gestures for the smallest infractions.

We need riders to obey traffic laws and respect cars, and motorists who respect the bicyclist's right to be on the road. A little of The Golden Rule would go a long way toward making the road safer for all of us. Sometimes riders make bad decisions and pay the price. A couple years ago, a longtime athlete misjudged oncoming traffic and was hit by a car and seriously injured. Not only was he hospitalized, but his brand new $4,000.00 bike was destroyed. Most of us who have biked for a long time have made poor decisions that could have resulted in serious injury, but fortunately did not. Ego and foolhardiness can get you in trouble. BE CAREFUL!

"Rode hard and put away wet"

18

Heroes

Many of the people I have met during my years of triathlon are worthy of respect, but the ones who stand out most in my mind are the ones who faced problems, yet been able to overcome those problems, and excel anyway. A few of these situations have been so extreme that little hope could exist, yet the person succeeded.

I have never met Lance Armstrong, but I hold him in more awe and respect than any other athlete, living or dead. What he has survived and overcome defies imagination. No novelist could have written a more improbable or more heroic scenario. His story is a real testament to the power of will and determination. Now that he has won a sixth Tour, he will always be remembered as one of the greatest athletes ever.

Another man I respect above most is my British climbing friend, Norman Croucher. Most people with an injury as severe as his, amputation of both legs just below the knees, would retire to a life of self pity and frustration. He did neither. He took stock of his situation, sought and used the help that was available to him, and became a world class climber capable of holding his own on any mountain with all but the very elite. On his first attempt at Aconcagua, he had broken one of his artificial legs while at base camp. While the rest of his group attempted Aconcagua, he climbed on one leg and crutches where possible, and crawled the rest of the way to the 16,800 ft summit of neighboring Ameghino. He did this solo, while hauling food and gear, over four days, and without a stove for heating food or drink. On his second attempt on Aconcagua, Norman was the first of the group, other than the guides, to reach the summit at 22,834 ft. The rest of us lagged behind even though we each had two natural legs. His determination, courage and positive attitude were an inspiration to me and caused me to rethink what is possible for all of us.

Norm Croucher and John Smolich
atop Aconcagua - 1982

My friend Jim Manfredo was involved in a deadly traffic accident which claimed the life of the friend he was riding with, and left Jim with a severely broken leg and in deep shock. The leg bone was put back together with a pin and required a second surgery to remove it. After recovering from the trauma, and the loss of his friend, he collected himself, had the second surgery done and a few months later, was able to go back to work and eventually, was able to run again. I have run with him since his recovery, and he is still a faster runner than me.

John Browning was told by his doctor that his athletic career was over due to a calcium buildup on a lumbar vertebrae. As John exited the transition area to begin the run on his last long race, he was doubled over from the pain in his back. A volunteer told him to get out of the runway because it was for athletes only. John informed the person that he *was* one of the athletes and was only trying to finish the race. He went on to win his age group. John sought medical treatment afterwards and found a physical therapist, shortened his races and training, and has completed six more years of sprint races.

Ron Ottaway had qualified for Ironman Hawaii, but developed two bad knees, both of which needed arthroscopic surgery. His surgeon wanted to do one first and later the other one. Ron told him there wasn't time for that, and had both done the same day. By that evening, he was on his treadmill, running. He was supporting most of his weight with his hands but none-the-less was going through the running motion just a few hours after surgery. Four months later, Ron finished second in his age group at Kona.

Larry Owens, Steve Meunier, John Devere, have all suffered and worked through injury and illness and maintained their fitness, when most others would have given up and retired to the easy chair. Annie Phillips lived with Chronic Fatigue Syndrome for months, yet perservered and is one of the best women in her age group in California.

These people who have done their best, gone through hard times, and returned to do their best again, are the real heros .

John and Emily Devere
on their wedding day

Final Thoughts

I hope readers have enjoyed this journal of the athletic part of my life. Hopefully the sense of fun, fellowship, adventure, and shared goals has come through, as well as the dedication and hard work that is essential for success. Triathlon has helped me stay fit and healthy, mentally as well as physically. If this writing has encouraged a few people to go out to exercise and maintain a healthy fitness level, my goals have been met. Nonetheless, it has been a pleasure to relive many of these moments, and that in itself has made the effort worth doing.

Let me end with a bit of Kerman wisdom: if you don't start out as a champion, just keep on going, you may outlive the competition.

Glossary

Triathlon - Any race incorporating three different diciplines into one event. Typically these are swimming, bicycling, and running, in that order. However, any sport may be exchanged for another, and there is no official order for the diciplines.

Biathlon - Any race having two diciplines.

Duathlon - A race with a run-bike-run format.

Adventure Race - A race involving several events and usually held in a remote area. Most races include some sort of water event, bicycling, running and hiking, some type of mountaineering, and orienteering. Duration of event can be from two hours to a week.

Sprint Triathlon - A race generally 0.3 mi swim, 14 mi bike, 3.1 mi run.

Olympic Triathlon - Approximately 0.9 mi swim, 24 mi bike, 6.2 mi run.

Long Course Triathlon - About 1.2 mi swim, 56 mi bike, 13.1 mi run.

Ultra Distance (including Ironman) - 2.4 mi swim, 112 mi bike, 26.2 mi run; there are a few double Ironman races, you do the math.

Wildflower Triathlons - Held annualy at Lake San Antonio, west of Paso Robles, CA. It is put on by TriCalifornia the first weekend of May and is called the "Woodstock of California." The Half Ironman and a Mt. Bike sprint race are held on Saturday and the Olympic distance is raced on Sunday.

Vineman Triathlon - Held annualy in Santa Rosa, CA. I have done both Half and Full Ironman races there.

Age Groups - Generally 16-19, 20-24, 25-29, 30-34, etc. until they run out of competitors. Some smaller races use 20-29, 30-39, etc. There are both male and female catagories.

Transition Area - A staging area where bikes are racked and eqipment is kept. This area is usually for athletes only in order to protect the equipment from pilferage. This is also where clothing and shoes are changed. In the early days some triathletes stripped down to the buff while changing, and now most races state somewhere in their rules that there will be no nudity in the transition areas. The race clock does't stop during a clothes change and most people practice their transitions in order to make it as fast as possible.

Aid Stations - Specific areas on the course at which water, sports drinks and sometimes food are officially passed to athletes.

Volunteers - Those good people who do the real dirty work that makes races happen, and who are seldom adequately thanked. Some of the bigger races need literally hundreds of volunteers who stand on the hot pavement in the sun for hours passing out water, collecting number tags, staffing the hospital tent, setting up, taking down, and a lot of other chores. A big *Thank You* to them all.

Drafting - Riding in an imaginary box two meters by seven meters behind another rider for more than a few seconds. Drafting during the swim is fine.

Time Penalties - Issued for various infractions such as drafting. Usually tacked onto your finish time. During the Ironman race in Hawaii, the guilty sit before they can start the run. Penalty times vary with the distance of the race. A drafting penalty in a sprint race might be 30 seconds, but three minutes in an Ironman.

Disqualification - The dreaded DQ. Short-cutting the course, abusive behavior, improper race number, no helmet, accepting unofficial help on the course; these can get you tossed out.

USAT - USA Triathlon. National governing board of triathlon. Certifies race courses, sets racing rules, provides insurance.

USTS - United States Triathlon Series. Onetime race producer, now defunct.

Photo Credits

Photos from the following people (and their collections) have been used throughout this book:

Phillip Bragg: *pg 3*
John Browning: *pg 105*
Sandra Browning: *pgs 81, 82, 86*
Holly Chohan: *pg 79*
John Devere: *pg 70*
Rick Feher: *pg 108*
Chuck Freuler: pgs 84, 93
Jim Goold: *pgs 10, 33, 36, 94, 96*
Jim Harris: *pgs 65, 76, 77*
Walter Hastings: *pg 9*
Rhonda Manfredo: *pg 73*
Trudi Manfredo: *pg 48*
Walter May: *pg 13*
Steve Meunier: *pgs 64, 72, 75*
Dan Montague: *pgs 2, 14, 19, 23, 25, 27, 28, 107*
Carter Nickel: *pg 44*
Dot Owens: *pgs 54, 78*
Ruth Russell: *pg 89*
Paul Slota: *pg 31*

Over the past 20 years of racing, there have been many people who have given me photos that were taken at the various events throughout the state. Most of the photos used in this book have been identified and the photographer named. There are a few photos reproduced here for which, unfortunately, I do not have the photographer's name, and so am unable to give the proper credit due. Some of those individuals who have contributed photos in the past include Jeff and Jenny Chadwick, Ray Avina, Barbara Anderson, Lee and Beth Case.

Early view of Aconcagua - 1982
(*photo: the author*)

Smolich and Croucher
discussing route of approach
march - Aconcagua, 1982
(photo: the author)

Tent view of Mercedario as seen from Aconcagua at 19,000 ft
(photo: John Smolich)

Summit - 22,834 ft
Back row: Norm Croucher, Ted Meyer, Dan Montague; *Middle row:* Mary Michel,
Ramon Rocca, Todd Marlatt; *Front row:* Vladimir Kovacevic, Paul Slota *(photo: John Smolich)*

The author displaying
frostbitten fingers
back at basecamp
(photo: Paul Slota)

On the bike at McFarland
(photo: Emily Devere)

Waiting for the start at Wildflower - 1992
(photo: Steve Meunier)

Wildflower
Left to right: Larry Owens, Dan Montague, Dot Owens, John Browning
(photo: Steve Meunier)

The *Phlying Phillips Phamily* with four tiles at Santa Barbara - 2002
(photo: Sandra Browning)

John Browning and the author: Santa Barbara winners - 2002
(photo: Sandra Browning)

Owl's Clover - one of the joys of Spring riding
(photo: the author)